A Life With God In It

Monika Schimunek

AuthorHouse™
1663 Liberty Drive, Suite 200
Bloomington, IN 47403
www.authorhouse.com
Phone: 1-800-839-8640

© 2008 Monika Schimunek. All rights reserved.

No part of this book may be reproduced, stored in a retrieval system, or transmitted by any means without the written permission of the author.

First published by AuthorHouse 8/26/2008

ISBN: 978-1-4389-0125-1 (sc)

Printed in the United States of America
Bloomington, Indiana

This book is printed on acid-free paper.

Introduction

Having had to grow up with the two most Powerful Religions that there are , one being the Jewish on my Mothers side, the other being the Catholic , there was not much different for us children, we could choose our own as we got older, which I did , Lutheran, , that was the one for me all my life . Mind you , learning from my Mother , all about her up bringing and from my Father too it did not hurt to know about the two most important religions from my Parents . Both of them where so modern for their age they left it up to us if we wanted to go learn about the Jewish community or the Catholic but for me it was enough to know about the Bible no matter what religion it would be thought in . My life has been a Roller Coaster from day one when I was born having been very sick for the first three months of my life I had to fight my whole life through against all odds but with the help of God made it thru , now this book is going to help some of the people who are going to read this but some of them it wont , they have to find their own way , everyone of us has to find their own way ,in Gods world there are so many ways , to make sure that whoever you are , you find your way ,the right way the way to God !

FOR THE LONGEST TIME , this subject was on my mind , having had so many experiences with the power of God , as they say , it needed to be written down .

How far back can anyone of you remember ,to their Childhood , to the time when they had been very young ,or when they where Teenagers ?

For myself it was to a time when I was very young , to be more specific ,two years old that is how far back I can remember . Only by the account of my Mother , she asked me one day , we had been talking about remembering , if I could remember a time that stuck in my mind . Yes to say the least , the thing that was so clear in my Memory was as follows .

My Mother had me on her hand while walking up to a bus stop near where we lived . We needed to wait for a bus , any Bus actually , my Memory was not too clear on the number of that Bus but the Man that got of at the Stop where we where waiting did stick in my mind , it was my Father . He had left to find work , it was then four years after the WW2. My Mother had taken me to the Bus Stop to pick him up never realizing that my Memory would be such to remember my Father by even describing what he was wearing and the big Duffel bag he carried ! Telling my Mom what I remembered , she shock her Head in disbelieve . How can you remember something like that, she said , the way you remember what he was wearing and that bag ! Still shacking her Head she went outside to tell my Dad who was feeding the chicken , by now, my age was thirteen and they had never talked about that day when my Father came back, telling us he had a Job . He did not say very much to me just picked me up and carried me home on his shoulders , something that stuck in my memory for all those years . Looking back now he seemed like a Giant to me, then of course he would to a two year old Girl ,right ? But the things that scared my Mom and Dad about my memory was that I could tell them some of the conversation they had while walking home .

It was then that I realized the power of God ,growing up at a time when Germany was being rebuild from next to nothing , having been born in 1947 there was not much for anyone to have or buy , but now we had everything . We had a House that my Dad build with my two brothers, also had a lot of Animal's for Meat . My Father had bought a few big Parcels of Land but that was never an interest of mine , the only thing that interested me was what bus to take to get to our Church ,we lived outside the City now , too far away to be walking all the time . It seemed to far for me any way ,but in reality it was only six Miles one way !

From early Childhood my Mother would always pray with me , every night, every morning .She had all these sayings out of the bible that she would cite to me ,as a small child one does really believe everything . When she was telling me about Jesus and God and how he let his Son be executed on the Cross , my believe ,somewhat ,got a bit less than before . For the longest time I could not get over that Story, about Easter, how Jesus arose from his tomb . But in time, my conviction towards God, and the Bible became more and more binding to me , never had some one told me that this would happen but it did . As long and as far as can be remembered , by me , there was always this Presents above , never had any one seen it but most of us do believe it is there. But I am getting ahead of myself, it was not easy for me to talk about this to anyone   some of the Children that grew up around our neighborhood   did not go to Church and the once who did where Catholics   we belonged to the Lutheran   Church , Evangelical   and most of my Friends later throughout my life, did not belong or believe the same as we did . What was very funny is as follows. My Mother grew up with Jewish believe and Lutheran , my Father was Catholic , both of their Parents did not want them to get Married, as a matter of fact , none of them where at their Wedding , till the day my Grandmother on my Mothers side died she did not talk to her Daughter any more, which was my Mom ! It was not nice never to have had Grandparents , my Dads Parents died during the War , my Moms Father too , the only one left was my Grandmother on my Mothers side but I never got to meet   here, only after she died did we find out that she had just lived half an hour drive away from us . That was somewhat of a shock to me , all my Friends where always telling   me about their Grandparents   after every weekend , Mondays at School   they told such nice stories about them , how nice they where and all the funny things they did with them and they would go in the summer Holidays to stay with them for the entire time . To me that always hurt somewhere inside and quite often talking to my Mother about this , blamed her for the fact that we did not have the pleasure of having Grandparents to go too . But , getting ahead of myself   is not so good , that is why   now we go back to growing up to be a Teenager . Most at the time my Mother did not have very much time for us Children, specially not for me, being the last of ten there was only my two year older Sister who was looking out for me. It was actually a good life by the time we had to go to School, my Sister had started only one year ahead of me since my Parents where told that I would be excepted at the age of five already in to first Grade we only where on class apart. In those days nobody went to School by bus or car all the Children walked to School, it was okay since there would always be some of the grown ups who came to pick some of us up at the end of Class time every day. Sometimes it was my Mother but most at the time someone else's Mother would be there just to make sure we did not get lost. After we had advanced in to the third Grade, there was nobody any more who would come to walk us home, we did not need anybody than any more either. So we though, but before leaving my house every morning we had to pray, it was not the longest prayer but very efficient, as it was about the day and the way home from School and how to be nice to all Children no matter what they looked like. That was an easy part because in those days there where no other children but German once, since every body stayed in their own Countries after the War nobody was permitted to live in Germany, neither would we be if we wanted to move to another Country outside of our own. Being that the way of life nobody thought anything of it, but we did have a lot of very poor Children. Some of them had to grow up without a Father or Mother since they died during the war, now they where living in Orphanages, they did not have the luxury of a Family who would look out for them. Finding out from some of the Children in my Class, some of their Parents would never come to visit, it seemed they had forgotten them. This is very hard for a Child to accept, specially at such a young age . It seemed we had it very good , having our own House, which my Father build with my two Brothers . We also had a lot of Land , could grow all kinds of Vegetables , we had two Pigs some Rabbits , Ducks , Geese and of course Chickens about twenty of each . It was not really a Farm , at least that's what my Dad always said , he called it his Hobby Farm . Any one who would ask me , was always told , that we do have a Farm , when one has more than thirty Animals no matter what kind , that is called a Farm . But what did it matter , we had a great life , living close to the Forest , we could go there and play ,having our Dog go with us whenever we went , besides that , our House was not far away from the Forest line and a Friend of my Fathers was the Forrester there . Everything was going great until my ninth Birthday , after the Cake was eaten and the children had to go home I got very sick and for two days could not walk , having pain in my belly . My Dad having been almost a Doctor , you see before the War, he was in the sixth year of Studies for Medicine but after the War he always told us that he had seen enough Blood to last him a life time . Never understood what he meant until growing up ,to about eighteen , then finding out all about the kind of things that went on during that awful time . When my Dad came home on the third day and my condition had not gotten better he phoned the doctor but to do that he had to walk to the front of our Road where they had a Phone Booth installed . In those days nobody had a phone , first of all one had to apply for it , and it could take up to two years before one would get that phone , but than it was also very expensive .Any way all that I could hear was my oldest Brother ,Harry had come , he came in to the Bedroom to look in on me but then was telling my Mom that may be she needs to go to the Hospital with me , "look Mom he said ," she is all green in her Face there is something very terrible wrong here, please get some clothes on her we take her to the Hospital . Being a Mother who always worried about her Children , my Mom did as he asked and put some clothes on me , but before my Brother could take me the Doctor had arrived . He was our old family doctor and made House calls , which in our days today are unheard of right ? All that was said as the Doctor walked in and took a look at me was , " put a blanket around her and bring her to my Car we have no time to loose , she is dying . Just the cry of my Mother made me open my eyes and look at here , I am not Mom promise . From than on the only thing that I later remembered was, after arriving at the Hospital was rushed up to the second Floor where the Operating rooms where and our Family doctor called the Nurses only to tell them they had to take that Woman who was in the OP out again and bring this Child in she is going to die if we do not Operate on her right now . After that it was dark for a few seconds or so but than there was this bright light and it was very warm . Walking along on a beautiful Garden it was very peaceful , a Dog came running towards me she was very nice looking very clean she liked my hand and wanted me to play with here . There where some People which I did not know but they did know me for some reason , than the one Man said to me , " it is so nice to finally met you we have waited such a long time to see one of our Grandchildren . That was hard to believe for a nine year old , my Heart was going a bit faster but the funny thing was , scared was not on the agenda at all , there was nothing to be scared off . Meeting some of the nicest People , one of them telling me that he was my oldest Brother , but telling him that could not be since Harry had just been at my Moms House he could not be here , or could he ? Another young woman told me that she was one of my Sisters and than there was this little girl who walked with me for a while , very blond hair green eyes she was very pretty , she took me by the hand telling me that she was so happy to see her big Sister . Turning around I asked her , which big sister is that , oh you silly she said , it is you ! That was all a bit much for me and I got very tired telling all of them that to sit down right now would be great, but was told by the one who was my Grandfather that I needed to go back , there is nothing to worry about he said , it is just that you do not belong her just yet you tell your Mom about us and tell her that we are all doing well and we are okay , will you do that ? Sure nothing easier than that but than all of a sudden it was dark again , where was the light , where was that wonderful Garden it was so nice there why did they send me back ? Feeling someone smacking me gently on my cheeks , my eyes opened , sitting next to my bed was my Mother , she had been crying a lot by the looks of her red eyes . She had such great eyes too , very dark but always warm looking when she looked at me . Thank God , you are awake she said , we had been very afraid for you do you know that , but why I asked . Well the Doctor had come out to let her know that there was little hope for me to wake up again , why they needed to operate on my was , my appendix had broken open three days prior to my being brought here , apparently the fluid that had come out from there had poisoned my whole body already , that was the reason my skin had turned this greenish color . But telling this to a nine year old was not so easy, but right in the middle of her wanting to tell me all of this I blurted out ," let me say hi to you from your Father and my two sisters , my brother was there too but it was not Harry , but he told me that he was my oldest brother . My little sister has great blond Hair and her eyes are just like the once from Dad . They had been walking with me in this wonderful Garden but then told me that you needed me back here more and may be one day we could get together again when it is my time . What did they mean by that Mom , my time , when is it my time ?Looking at my Mothers face , she had turned very white , Dad come in here she was calling , my Dad had been waiting outside the Room they had been permitted only one of the Parents to visit me because they believed that I needed the rest . There was no rest that was needed but answers from both of my parents . As my Dad walked in my Mom asked me to tell him what just was told to here, so telling him exactly as before , he too was not looking to great , how can you say this he said what did your Grandfather look like ? Describing him in full detail to both of my parents also my brother and my two sisters they looked at one another than started crying . What had I done , just wanted you to know what they told me I said very quietly , Mom bending over giving me a big hug than telling me , it is okay , it is just that we had never told you about the brother and sisters you had before you where born they died during the War you would never now them because we have no pictures of them left , all was destroyed in the fires from the Bombing . Knowing that it was okay to tell them about all those People that where there it was fun to describe them in full detail, while they where shaking their heads once in a while and saying , we can not believe this , but than telling me ,you know that you had been given the greatest gift anyone could ever get , you got to see the People we loved most before you came along , nobody knew what they looked like any more not even we did for sure but God gave you the opportunity to see them to know that he is there he truly exists in our daily life and you had been given this to strengthen your believe . We could tell that he had been doubting some of the things we had thought you about the Bible because of all the things that we are now finding out about the War and you are getting older and understanding more about things like that is going to be very hard to believe for you . But God knew that so he gave you this meeting with them to see what he can do for you and how much he loves you , does he love me more than you or Dad ? Of course he does he loves all of us much more than we ever could love another Person he is so full of love for all his Children , because that is what we are , without God there is nothing , without him nothing will grow , there will be no peace on Earth nothing that we could look forward too . But you need to sleep now , we can talk about this when you come home , okay ? Both of them giving me a big hug but before they went out of the Room I bend over the bed corner telling my Mom , my tummy hurts I do not feel to good may be you should stay , with that bending outside the bed even more and then it all came out , vomit , that's what it was , because in those days they gave to much of this horrible stuff that they put one to sleep with called aether . Any way , now believing that the Nurse will come in an scold me because I spit on her nice clean Floor , that did not happen , to my surprise she was telling,' me what a good Girl you are ', this is good at least you did not get all the linens dirty . So that was the thing, it was better just to mop the floor than having to take all the bedding off and putting new once on . Today the things that I had learned would be with me for the rest of my Life, not realizing that many

more of those surprise happenings would be coming my way . Not that I was or am an Angel by far not so , but trying to behave like my Mother always told me to behave was not easy for me either , on one hand there was my believe in God , knowing what he wanted of me , not to kill anybody or steal from anyone , not to sleep with my Neighbors Husband or say bad things about them , those where things that where easy for me to uphold but the rest was not so easy . After coming home from the Hospital we had a good talk in which they told me not to tell anybody besides them what experience was behind me the things that where told and said would be best kept to myself , my Mom told me that nobody else would probably believe anything that was said . Why not , this was a question that would soon be answered to me by one of my Friends a Catholic Girl , not that it mattered to me who she was we liked one another and went to School together every day, once in a while she asked me to go to church with her on a week day .

After asking my Parents about that, was told that it did not matter where I would say my Prayers as long as I did not loose the perspective of God , it was all about him and not the Catholics or the Evangelists . She was right of course , over the years it became clear to me that she always had been right when telling me about the bible . One day as a lot of us Girls got together in my back yard the temptation was to great as to pass up this time . Telling them as we where sitting around under the Apple tree what had happened to me while in the Hospital believing that all of them would understand , the things that needed to be told, if only to know that People would believe . But that was the biggest mistake ,or one of the biggest once in my life . After having finished telling them all most all of them started to laugh very much , the rest of them just got up , one of the Girls even telling me that her Mother had always told her that I was crazy and she should not play with me any more . Several of those Girl went as far as to beat me up one day while coming home from School, there where five of those that used to be my Friends or at least that's what they had told me they where , now it would be proven other wise and not thru . Arriving at home my Mother saw right away that something had happened asking me to tell her everything ,well Mom , you where right , nobody believed me when told what had happened to me at the Hospital most of them do not speak to me any more and the rest just beat me up to day !

You should have listened to me my Girl , whipping the blood of my face that had run down from my eyebrow ,she gently cleaned the rest of my face , you are such a lovely Girl why did you have to go and tell them , knowing what had happened to you for us is wonderful but for strangers who do not truly believe in God , is very hard to understand

. But why is that so , looking at here asking her this question I needed to know why it is such a big deal for People to understand that there is a Haven to which we all will be going , well , may be not all of us , but most . My Mother always knew the right thing to say and do she just told me and made me promise not to tell anyone any more about those things because she said , "after the War nobody wants to hear about some good things, most People are still very mad of the outcome of that War , now if you tell them this Story they pretend not to believe it because that is what they want to make themselves believe . It would be best for all not to talk about that at all any more okay ?

Yes Mom if you feel that way than that is the way it is going to be done . That's my Girl she said giving me a big hug , now one has to know that hugs where not given very freely in our Family only on special occasions which this was today since being beaten up it felt good to feel Moms arms around me . One year later my Brother Harry wanted me to come in the Summer Holidays to his House to spend with my nice and nephew , my nice was only five years younger than me , her Brother was only one year old . My Brother and his wife Maria had four Children all in the time of 16 years , so every four years they had another Child . Three Girls one Boy ,who they named Harry junior . Looking nothing like my Brother who was dark haired and had the same dark eyes as my Mom , where his Son was very blonde and had blue eyes almost green like my little Sister that I had met that faithful day at the Hospital . As a matter of fact telling my Brother about that he smiled than told me that he has had almost the same experience during the war . He was only seventeen when he was called to the Hitler Jugend , but there was no way out , he had to go and so did my other

Brother Helmut who was only fifteen at that time . Never understood why that was , why children had to fight for a Country that nobody wanted to fight for in the first place , just some crazy Guy who wanted to own the whole world .What a stupid idea ,he could not have been very smart or he would have realized that nobody can take the place of God , at ten years old that was what I was thinking . As my Mom asked me if that would be okay to stay with Harry for three weeks thinking of how much love my Brother always had shown me there was not doubt that it was okay with me to stay at his house . The first nice surprise when getting there was , he had build a Kite for me , one with my favorite colors which at that time where blue , as the sky , white as the little sheep clouds . and very red as the blood of Jesus that he gave for me too . It was a great kite and having unpacked asking my mother if it would be okay for me to go outside to fly this kite , it was okay with her but my little nice , Rosemarie was coming with me , she insisted . Now to a ten year old this was not the best decision to take a five year old along ,but she started to cry and since that was always one of my weak points not being able to say no to some one who was crying , she could go with me . But mind the Weather, Mom said , the clouds do not look like it is going to stay this nice there might be a thunder storm brewing somewhere . If you see it getting a bit darker out side, please come in right away okay ?

    Promise , I will come in right away if there is any sign of a Thunder Storm Mom. That was it and off we went , just being happy that the baby did not need to come with me too but then it was kind of nice having my nice there with me she was telling me all the things she had done in Kindergarten and what they had been talking about . She was turning very quiet all of a sudden which made me look at her closely , why are you so quiet now , " well I am scared she told me , what on earth for there is nothing to be scared about at flying a kite, it is very easy . No , not that she said , but the teacher told us that we are all going to hell if we do not do exactly as the Bible tells us . That was news to me and this was one of the times when the feeling came over me to go and hit that Teacher over the head with a stick of some kind . What a dumb thing to tell you ,looking at her my kite lying on the Ground , that Teacher of yours does not know what she is talking about , you will not go to Hell at all , most of us are going to Heaven , there are going to be some People who will not go there but that is for God to decide not for us down here and certainly not for a stupid Teacher like yours . Very seldom did I use any kind of swear but this stupid came right out of my heart , and looking upwards to the sky , sorry God for this word but since you can not be down here right now it was what I felt ,please forgive me . My nice was looking at me as if I was a Ghost , who are you talking to she said , there is nobody there , oh yes there is just look up he is always up there looking down to us if we are doing good or not he never would want anyone to tell you that you are going to Hell ." How can you be so sure she said , last Sunday in church the Pastor said the same thing to us , Mommy and Daddy where there too just ask them they can tell you this is thru . Well , when we get home that is just what we will do since my Mom is here she can set you all straight . Convinced that my Mother would be able to set anybody straight on this subject it was time to fly the kite , now you hold on to the tail , handing it over to my nice she knew what was meant , going away from her for a few yards than started to run by calling out to her ," now let go of the tail the kite needs to fly ! We had that kite in the air for quite some time just enjoying the flight of it and the colors against the blue sky , but all of a sudden the sky turned a bit green and grey the sun had gone too, very fast , it is time to get the kite down , you can run home already and tell them that as soon as the kite is down I will be coming too , okay ? Sure she said , she only needed to go across the Field and then cross over a walkway but not a Road , besides most People around here just had Bicycles there where hardly any Cars since my Brother lived out in the country just like we did except he was living about two hour Car ride from where we lived . Any way she started to run home ,when I noticed that my kite had got coughed up in a High wire Electrical line . Well that is special , talking to myself had become second nature ,since loosing a lot of the so called Friends by telling them the thru story that had happened to me . But not to despair , always was told that no matter how much or how the kite would be coughed up never try to bring it down you will be electrified if you do , but naturally at ten years old that is not an option if one wanted this kite so badly back right ? Not with me any way , looking up to the sky starting to talk to God once more asking him to let me have my kite , that for that he could be sure to see me in church with my brother next Sunday , knowing full well that God does not make any deals with anyone no matter what , still started pulling on the string to bring my kite down when hearing someone calling my name telling me to let go of the string , do not bring your kite down you wont survive that , it was my brother Harry he came running towards me while I still kept on pulling that string and sure enough, there the kite came down, not having gotten hurt at all ,was happy showing off the kite to him , " see , it came down , there is nobody hurt , it is as if God had answered my request to let me have my kite back . Harry put his arms around me , " promise me one thing he said , never do this kind of thing again , can you promise me that ?But nothing happened to me or the kite , "still he said , you have to promise me one thing , never to do this again ! Okay , if that is what you want than yes here is my promise , but why are you so scared now nothing has happened to me , that is just it he said , but may be next time it will . Having lost three of my siblings already there is nothing that can bring them back but I can watch over you if near to you , after all , you are my baby sister and the thought of may be loosing you is unbearable to me . Well , if that is how you feel than yes , with this I promise never to do this again , giving him a big hug and a kiss on his cheek we walked towards his House . He did not tell my Mom about that incident may be that was a good thing , to this day there is no way of knowing for sure but to me it was God telling me , it is okay this time but next time you have to leave it okay ? That was okay with me too, most of all now thinking about the fact that the Electricity in that High wire Cable could have burned me to a crisp was not a very nice way of looking at . However one is going about daily life there will always bee an incident where one has to make a choice , if it is the right one , well that is another story but by making that choice one can only learn and there is nothing lost , nothing at all . Considering the fact, that when we grow up we do not think about God to much any more because there are so many distractions along the way . We meet a new Friend or our first boy friend . Or, we meet our future Husbands or Wife ,but there is very little thought about God in all of that to most People, but I guess this one here is not like most People but rather very different from them . Having always been told by a lot of People that one is very strange while talking to one self, it is easy to believe that those who say that all the time, may be right ! But than on the other hand , they could be dead wrong too . For one person like me there is always the morning Prayer as well as the night time one even if there have been some times in my Life where I did not want to talk to God because I believed that he had forgotten me completely ,of course he had not . At the age of thirteen having had some experiences about what to tell Friends or so called , one got very careful what to say any more . Most People that we knew may there been Friends or family they thought that there was something wrong with me because of my conviction , no matter what anyone else said I knew better and most times the outcome was such that they had to give me the benefit of a doubt . Walking down to our Church every Sunday was not easy, since being the only one who would go to Church . My Sisters where much older than me besides they thought me to be some kind of crazy nut as well and left no opportunity out to tell me so , that is why to this day we do not have a very nice relationship . Actually it has never been very important to me to get along better with my Sisters , my Mom was the person that was mostly on my side , my Dad as well . Both knew very well the things that my Sisters did to me or said but they let us deal with that which we always did . Now as a Teenager it was very important to me to find out who is truly my Friend , one more year means the end of School for me and some of my Classmates ,there are a few who have to repeat the class but lucky for me my best friend Ursula was not one of them . We both started the same job at the same time at a Textile Factory , the main reason was to become an invisible mender , which meant to be able to mend any fabric that was produced at this factory it would take us three years to learn that trade . There was good money in it but in those days one would give all the money to the Parents since they where the once who looked after our Hope Chest , as they call it here , also they paid all the bills so needless to say the money we made was theirs by right in those days . Nobody did mind either since we all had to give the Money to our Parents there was no difference between any one of us , the only thing was that even to learn invisible mending we made more money than most Girls at our age just because it was such a sought after job to be learned by the Textile industry . We always took the same bus in the morning also in the evening if Ursula was not there one day I would stay longer , it was very good if we could do that and came Pay day we found an extra bill or two in our pay . In those times there was no such thing as having the Money transferred in to a Bank account one got a yellow envelope with cash in it also the hours that we had worked , if there was overtime we got paid extra for that but most at the time we did not work over time . My Parents where always very protective of me since the bus stop was about twenty minutes away from our house they wanted me to come home in day light . That was okay in the summer time but in the winter it proved to be a bit more difficult , because the darkness would set in around five in the afternoon ,which was exactly the time we where off work . Several Girls came from my neighborhood but not directly from the Street that we lived , most of them only walked two minutes till home where my way took about twenty . Sometimes our Boss would come to ask if anyone of us could stay later, there would be an extra bonus in it for the once who would ,knowing that my Parents always could use some extra money

I would stay late . As it happened we found out that there was a Rapist going around in our Neighborhood he had already got two women , but the Police could not catch him . One has to know that the bus stop was about a mile away from my house , from the place where we all got off it was one street , than there was an area where there was a Playground on the left hand side the other side was just a park kind of area ,nobody ever walked there it was to wild overgrown with thistles . Since my parents found out about that rapist they had told me not to come in the dark any more, but as it happened we needed to get some of the fabrics out by the next day and being September it was dark already by five so it made no difference to me to work longer hours it still would be dark . One of my Friends had gone to let my Parents know that I would be on the last bus , which was ten o'clock , at night . Needless to say both my Parents where not to happy with me that day because after all there was danger waiting around the dark corner between the two streets , it was precisely the area where those other two women had been attacked . Now sitting on the last bus going home , like most times I was talking to God , telling him how nice it would be for my Mom to get this extra bonus she needed to go to the Hairdresser , she had not gone for years , there never seemed enough Money for her to do anything . But my next pay check would be good for her to get , also God , please let me get home okay you know that dark corner around the playground when going past there , please let there be no danger for me . The prayer went on until my stop , the bus driver knew most of us Girls we always where the same crowd that got on the bus and off on the same stop , so that night he asked me to be very careful , may be you could ask one of the People living close to the playground to accompany you just till you got past there okay .?

May be that is not such a bad idea , thank you for your concern but my Dad probably is going to come to pick me up . What I did not know at this time was , my Father had to work late that day ,he just got home a few minutes before I was getting of the bus . Besides he did not know then that his Daughter would come with the last bus , but my mom told him right away , meanwhile walking through the first Street was okay there where some Street lights mind you not the nice once we have today , no , the yellow light looking kind that would only be every quarter mile . Any way , at this moment there was not time to be scared , walking quit fast like always with my long legs , came to the last house before the Playground area . Should I ask those People if one of them would go with me just past there , well it was worth a try , but as so many times in our lives , if one needs someone there is nobody there . It was like in most neighborhoods where every body knew the other Person, so the Lady of the house opened the door , hi Monika she said can we help you with anything ? Yes , if your son could just go with me to the other side of the Playground area that would be great , my Dad is probably coming towards me from the other end he will meet me at the front end of our street ! So sorry , she said , but Christopher is still in the Gym , my Husband has night shift he left about two hours ago it is just me that is home but to be honest , there is no way that I could go with you it would mean coming back alone , you understand that ,don't you ?

Sure I do not to worry , besides I got my little scissor in my right hand pocket it will be okay , thank you any way .With that, leaving her front step I went on to cross that dark area , there was not a Street light until the beginning of the street we lived on ,which was about one hundred feet from this last house . Having never been able to walk slow made my way over to cross walking fast having my hand around my scissor still talking to God and feeling not so scared right now , when all of a sudden I could hear foot steps coming from the left side of me . That was where the Playground was ,it was clear to hear because they only had Gravel on that surface the crunch was what made me hear it . Now starting to say , God let me be fast enough to outrun this Bastard , that word I had heard from my Dad ,which was unusual he never used swear words honestly , never . But while starting to run the other Footsteps would start running to , this must be a good runner I thought still not being to scared since God was here with me there was no reason to be this time , that Guy whoever he was , would not get away with his attack . When we had Track running in School I was always one of the best once ,having more legs than body it was easy for me, so running was second nature to me . Having reached the beginning of our Street there was the first Street light and having to make sure that the Guy or whoever it was did not follow me any more turned around just very fast , only to see that , it was a Guy and I knew him he lived in our Street ,first thinking that I might be running from him was very silly but then saw his face . It had changed from what I was used to see on him , something in my gut told me to run as fast as was possible . While running towards our house which was at the very end of this Street could hear him breathe down my neck almost , which made me run faster , while hearing him call out to me , I get you if not tonight there will be another time but I get you !

So much for that now the fear started setting in but then there was someone coming towards me and a shadow run right past me , it was our German Sheppard , my Dad had after my Mom had told him that I would be on the last bus , let our Sheppard out which he never did . But since the Dog had never run away from the Property he thought it would be a good idea to have him loose so when he wanted to pick me up he did not have to go to get the Dog , which was to the back of the house and would have taken some valuable minutes . That moment I heard someone call out , Help , Help , take this Dog of me he is going to kill me , oh no he won't my Dad said , but I will . No Dad going back to where he was , told him that all is well, he did not get me but he told me he would may be tomorrow or another night !

He won't I promise you this , my Dad said we see to it that he is put away for a long time believe me . Than he realized who he had coughed , why on earth have you been doing this , it was not something that one wanted to listen to , besides by now my Brother Harry who had been visiting this afternoon was still here and had taken me by the arm walking me home while my dad and one of the neighbors where waiting for the Police to arrive to take this Man to Jail, where he was put for twelve years . The very sad part about that was that he had raped a woman who was Pregnant , when her baby was born it was blind somehow it had a lot to do with the attack . But what was even worst was , he had five Children and sometimes we would baby sit his Children he was well known and worked in a Bank . After that night , there was nothing that his Family could do from keeping some of the People around our street to harassing them every day , their Children would be pushed of the side walk, some threw rocks at their house and windows ,until one day we saw the Moving Van parked outside their House . My Parents always liked the Woman she would come and get Eggs and Vegetables from my Mom , the Children would be at our House a lot because we where baby sitting them . Any way it was a sad good by , we had invited her and the Children to come over for a last meal, my sister was helping her packing while the kids would be at our house for me to look after . From that time on we got to know who was a good person and who was not , the once who go to church every Sunday and sometimes during the week , where the once who shunned her most , gave her the most problems, it was very sad because neither she nor her kids could help what their father did . Having always been very fortuned to have Parents that would tell me exactly what to do and what the best way of life was ,I could see what kind of People we where living next too . On the other hand , my Mother always told me not to judge any body else , just look at your self she said and see how many mistakes you make in your life after that you have found out that nobody is perfect and God does not want you to be a Judge , he is the one who will make everything right as it should be . A few years after this incident with the Rapist , we had almost forgotten what had expired when we got a Post card from that Man , telling us how very sorry he was to have done what he did , he also send the other two woman the same Cards . When on that following weekend my Mom asked me to go with her to the Woman and her Children just to bring them some fresh Eggs some items out of our big Garden , also some Chicken and a Goose . Arriving at the place where she lived now with her five kids we rang the door bell , when she opened the door to let us in she had been crying , please come in she said ,going upstairs where she walked right past the door to leave it open for us we could not understand what was going on . After giving her all the things we had brought for her she asked us if we would like to sit and have a coffee with her , and loving coffee already at that time , looking at my Mom , we said yes. Naturally my Mother wanted to know what was going on with her , "well she said ,'my husband will be released in one year , because of good behavior he is getting out to go to work for us , they found that he is no good for us behind bars but if he can go to work that would be good but nobody is going to give him a job . The only one he would be able to get is as a Cab driver , but he is a Banker not a Taxi Driver you know he does not mind , after visiting him the other day he told me that he would do anything to make things right for all of us he even would go and clean Bathrooms if that is what he needed to do . He also agreed to have this Operation done so he would never do the kind of thing ever again , but the worst thing is , my twin sons do not want him to come home any more , they told me if he sets one foot in this House the throw him out . What can I do , " turning to my Mom , can you tell me what to do, having had not sleep last night and waking up with this very bad headache , she said , fighting with my boys has given me such a stomach upset but I still do not know what to do . Loosing two of my children is not an option ,I could never let that happen but also giving my Husband one more chance is what needs to be done , can you see what the problem is now ?

Sure we can , my Mom said to her but you have to make sure that your sons know exactly what to expect when your Husband comes back home , they have to be told that he will be the head of the Family again ,one they would have to listen too , also that every body deserves to have a second chance given, it is very important for your Husband to get this chance don't you think so ? That is what I told my Children this morning but none of them want him here , they still remember to much about that time before we moved away from your street , remember that she asked ? Only all to well , my Mother said but you and they , have to put this behind you once and for all, we can help you if you need to talk to anybody, please do not hesitate to phone me okay ? Well my Mom said after going back to the Car , this is going to be hard on all of them we have to Pray for them but most of all they all have to pray for themselves or it won't work out , only God can help them to put that Family back together again ! More times than not , did my Mom impress me with her believe she did not waiver , there was no may be about her believe in God she knew what he could do and she believed so strongly that there was nothing any one could say to sway her away from that . Often my wish was that my believe would be as strong as hers having very much respect for both of my parents because they always said they would do something and they did , never was there a may be always a yes we can do it . Still going every Sunday to Church but now having some company with me to walk down there , this Family would come by bus to our street and together we walk down to our church , coming back home they would have Dinner with us than go on the bus back home . None of our Neighbors where talking to us for some time, after having seen that we would care for them but after a while one or the other would come to our house , if only being nosy at first but then beginning to see that my Mother did not care whether they liked what she was doing or not she would keep on doing what she always had done , helping anybody who needed help . Years went by and the

Husband was a model citizen his Children had come to grips with the things he had done not understanding them but seeing that now was now and the past was behind them , he was a very good Father and one of his Sons became a very good Lawyer his two Daughters became Teachers the other two boys went to the Army and Navy . There was only one example of what God can do if you trust in him he can make any wrong right again just give him a chance , let him take over your life and you will find that you can be much happier than you had been before .

    Being almost eighteen , now there was a bit of forgetting to pray every day , oh not that it was forgotten completely but some days it was other days just a fast few seconds , it was a time when all went so good for me never anything went wrong   still living with my Parents , that's what we all did in those days . Nobody was moving out until after they got Married ,but in my case , loving to be home with my Mom & Dad always telling them that this Daughter would not be moving out at all , I like to stay with you forever   , well my Dad said one day , we heard that before but now look most all of you are gone just you and your sister are still here , not that we are complaining but just saying that nobody stays home forever ! Well than this one will be the first , having said that , my mom asked me how my Boyfriend was , he was the son of my Mothers best Friend and both Mothers where very glad that this was so . We had been seeing each other for three years when I got pregnant , nobody was as happy as our Parents but there was a niche , I did not want to get Married , it took my Mother all but eight months to convince me that the best way for all of us was that the Father of my child and I should get married . Now never having been one of those children who oppose their Parents finally gave in and four weeks before my Daughter was born, we got married just in time for her arrival . It was funny since all the friends and neighbors knew that there was a baby on the way ,we did make no secret about that . But with all intended purposes we did love each other and when the baby came it was a Girl , we where quite happy even if my Husband was working out of Town most at the time , he was an Electrician and worked for a Company that installed High wire Power lines . Life was good , very good , since my parents had a big House , we got to live upstairs in a two bedroom apartment , the best thing about that was I could go out in to the Garden and get fresh vegetables or fruits any time I wanted to . Like I said it was great but the only thing was when one is very happy and all goes well we forget some one , God , we do not think about to pray every day any more , why should we, all is well with the world there is not need for him to do anything for us , or is there ?One day I found out that there is a need at all times good or bad ,it does not matter but there is a need to talk to him or at least there should be . As life went very well we got a second Child this time it was a boy , both of my children where born in my Parents house since there was no need for me to go to the Hospital we had the Midwife and the Doctor come to the House which was great so right after the birth I could go take a shower which I did both times . Everything should have been very good if not for the fact that my beloved Mother got very ill , she had her first Heart attack . Now began a time for me where God was again my best friend but he had another life in mind for me, today I know that but then ! Any way not only was my Husband always gone but my Mother who had come home from the Hospital needed more help now than ever , she was not permitted to do very much hard work any more like she used to do so the Garden and Laundry and cleaning of the House became my job . Not that I needed to do that , my dad wanted a cleaning Lady to come in help with all of the chores but my Mom did not want a stranger in her House , and as we lived just upstairs it was easy for me to help . Gladly did so too , because remembering all the good times we had with my Mother all the things she did for me but not only that she did for everybody, it was time that we now would do all we could to help her out . At least that was my believe , my sisters did not think the same way as they told me plain out , " we can not come to help , first of all we do not have cars second we can not spare the time to be up there for the whole day, neither for just half a day . That took care of that , my Dad came upstairs this one day just to let me know that my oldest Sister had just come she would like to talk to me about looking after Mom , "could you please come down stairs he said , she wants to talk to you . Why can't she come upstairs , I am right in the middle of cooking the children's Lunch . Okay I will let her know he said than turning around to go down to let my sister know what was said . It did not take her long to come to see me, she was not very happy with the fact that she had to come to see me instead of the other way around but for me that did not really matter ,specially not now or today I should say because having been up since five this morning tending my Moms Vegetable Garden picking Cucumbers for pickling , tomatoes ,peas and some other kinds by now there was no small wonder getting tired had a reason . But she did not see it that way , so what she said , you had been working in the garden since five this morning , this is my lunch break and you have to stop asking me to look after Mom ,there is no time in my Day so please stop phoning me it is not going to happen . Like I told Dad already you will be the one who needs to do all of this from now on . Well that was good to hear not that it did matter to me , for me to do this for my Mother it would be okay, having come so far to help with everything it was okay do keep it up . Those where hard Years, the second Heart attack came about one year later , all had been going so well with my Mom but one day she believed she could help outside hanging up her bedding , we did not have a Dryer or washer , all was done by hand . When my Dad build this House he also build a big Cement Kettle down in the basement which as an insert had a copper kettle, underneath one could light a fire than the linens and all the white laundry pieces would be cooked for about an hour , after that we put them in smaller tubs to cool down at the end they would be put through one of those old wringers, and after that brought out to be hung to dry in the wind . For one year all went well, every Monday was put aside for just doing the Laundry and taking of all the bedding in the whole house . Now my two year old sister was still living in this same house but when there was work she was never to be seen , she either needed to go out to shop or to see somebody . Which to my Dad seemed very funny because she never went anywhere if there was not a big job to be done ,but as soon as she found out this was one day there would be a lot of work she disappeared .Some of our neighbors who would drop in to see my Mom how she was doing and so on, asked me a lot of times why none of my Sisters where here to help me but to me that was no subject , all the help my Mom needed she got from me no matter what . My two children would be outside with me when weeding the garden or picking the fruit or feeding the Animals when my Dad was not home from work yet

. Being an Engineer he never had just a eight to five job , there would be some emergencies with some of the Clients of his Company where he was requested to come himself, but the Animals never had to go hungry, my kids loved to throw them the kernels of their food and could not say enough about how funny it looked some of them fighting for a few morsels . Mostly Claudia my daughter would talk at this time, Dieter was not to eager to talk . But lets not get away from this life , we had it very good until one day my Husband had come home from one of his trips, to tell me that he had been transferred to a different City about an hour drive away from here . Now that was not such good news , hopefully we would not have to move there , asking him right away about that .

Well he said , " we do have to move there because he would be the new Manager for a Crew of twenty People and needed to be close enough to always be on call . The reason he had accepted that position was that he wanted to be near his Family now and not always out and about . That was understandable to Monika ,but what about her Mother she needed help and did not want strangers to come in to her house as she had said many times before , she needed her Daughter to be there for her . Knowing that and keeping that in mind he said to his wife ,"you can always come down here by Train during the day and I pick you up on my way home, since our head office is still here it is no problem for me to come by your Parents house to pick you and the kids up . For all things to happen all at once finding out the very next day that we would have another Child , I was pregnant again and it would not be easy for me to come here every day . What to do , it was a big problem so it seemed any way but on a lighter note it was not . Having so much faith had its good points , talking to God about all of this had given them the incentive to go about daily life as planned , Monika would come every day by bus and train to her Moms house at night her Husband would pick her up to take all of them home . As it is always better planning than doing so was this one , first of all the Apartment we had to move in to was not very nice , meaning the surrounding was not very nice ,the place was like a Cement palace the whole building looked like a box nothing special . This was something I would have never moved in to if my life depended on this , besides that we now had to live on the second Floor of this cement box , there was this small Balcony but it would not be good to leave the children to play out there by themselves it was short enough for them to climb up on and fall over . No , by no means was this a good place to raise children but as my Husband promised me it was only for a short time he would be eligible for a Company Apartment in my home town we just had to wait a few months . Well , that was some good news but telling my Mom and Dad about this would not be easy , they had depended on us or me to stay there to look after my Mother what now ? Moving with all the furniture and the two children was not so easy , we did not have a lot of Money to pay for a Moving truck or crew , so naturally we moved our self . Having help from my two brothers it was not as bad as we first believed the apartment was nice all big rooms two children's bed rooms one for us and than of course kitchen , living room and the bathroom was nice and big , if it had not been for the fact that this looked like a cement jungle outside it would have been perfect . But then who ever said that anything would be perfect in anybody's life ? Nobody ever told me that , so we had to make the best of it

, for the first few months it was okay to travel to my Parents house it took me two and half hour every day first to walk to the bus stop was ten minutes but than twenty five to get to the Train station , from there it was over one hour ride to my Hometown then another twenty minutes by bus to the closest stop and a fifteen minute walk with the two children . Lucky for me that they both could sit in the carriage or it would have been quite heavy to carry either one of them . Going in to my seventh month there where complications with my pregnancy , the Doctor that we went to told me that they should take my child, now ,by Caesarean section but that was not an option for me , insisting on another Doctors opinion , went to my hometown with the children the next day only to be told ," you should not have had any children as you have been told from the first pregnancy , but you did not listen, now you are going to have your third child and it is not going to be easy to carry this one for the whole term so , I suggest that you come back her to live and stay of your feet for at least the last few months okay ". That was my own Doctor , the one who was looking after me from the first time , now this was not so good what about my Mother I asked myself , it was not easy letting someone else look after her she had been in the Hospital once again in between now she was home again what would she say about all of this ? Nothing is ever going to be easy for me in my life ,there has always been some kind of turmoil but now this was to much we just had move to the other place six month ago, we have to move back how would that go there was no way we could get an apartment that fast . But as always God has his own plan with us , forgetting to pray for his help he did any way . In a way that was funny really , on my way to my Moms house I was thinking of an easy way to tell her that my sister would look after her for the next few months , but did not want to tell her about the outcome of my Doctors visit it would just upset her too much , taking that chance would not be an option for me . However like it has always been faith had her own time of doing things this time she was telling me that all would be well just count on God , which I did and he did not disappoint me in the least . My husband came to pick me up at my moms house and in the Car started to tell me that we could move to my home town and close to my parents house by next weekend , he had already asked some of his buddies to come out and help with the move . That was great news to me but now needed to let my husband know what the Doctor had said about this pregnancy .He just looked at me and said ," if that is the case than you will stay of your feet I can get some holidays for about a month after that we see what comes next okay ? No it was not okay , one thing was for sure , if he would stay home for a month he would have to miss the one week when the baby would be born meaning he would be out in some other City not being able to come home for the birth . It will be okay he said just believe me okay , all will be well , promise . Coming weekend we had a lot of people helping us it was very nice there was nothing that needed to be carried by me just look after the children my husband said to me , that was an easy task ,the tow of them where not only the best looking children from all of the other once who are around but they also where the best behaved once , both of them where very happy to have a little sister or brother and we spend a lot of time finding names for either one gender . The new apartment was again on the second floor but the Doctor had told me not to walk up or down some stairs . Not telling him right away would be the best way to

do this , but one night having a lot of pain and being afraid of loosing the child , found my way to God once more , in the past few months had forgotten all about him ,now it was almost time for the baby to be born just two more weeks , this is why , I did not want to lose it now . Sitting in my kitchen while the other two children where asleep already , my husband was send out two days ago to another City , the prayer started like this ," dear God you probably are mad at me for not talking to you sooner , or not talking to you enough, but right now your help is needed very much needed ". Making you a promise to never forget to pray and always teaching my children to do the same , but please now you need to help me . This pain, is almost un bearable there is nothing that anybody else can do , only you are the one who can help me here and now , please do not be mad at me any more and help me !" Naturally this was not the first time that the prayer was only because I needed help, but most at the time if praying always would include all my children , my Mother and Father my other siblings and my husband for all to be kept save and healthy . Until now it all worked out fine to this night , hopefully he was not too mad at me any more , that was my thinking but the answer came about half an hour later , the pain stopped totally sitting in the kitchen with my feet up on another chair this felt good no more of the cramp like feeling that went all the way from my Stomach to my back and around again never to stop even for one second , but now , it was gone , thank you God for listening to me . That night going to bed there was another prayer that only was between me and him nobody would know about that until this Book . Knowing that my baby's' live was at stake the prayer was as follows . " All mighty God who reigns over Heaven and Earth I thank you from my whole Heart , but still have to ask for some more favors from you , please let my baby be healthy and strong enough to come out of my womb on his own , everybody has been telling me that it would have been better for me not to have had any children at all , you have given me three tremendous gifts which are appreciated so much by me , the promise that I give you in turn is , always be there for my children , never let any harm befall them no matter what , making sure they always have a good home and good Mother , whit that I need your help too , you have to show me how to be a good mom to them for as long as they need me okay ? But most of all . keep them save when I am not around help them in their decisions that they have to make when they grew up and please let me never loose their love as they will never loose mine .Please let my mother see this new baby, let her be with us for a bit longer I pray this in Jesus name , amen . Never had one prayer come so deep from the heart as this one , my children where all that truly matter to me , spending so much time with them every day there was no way to imagine having not have them in my life it would not be good ,God knew that , this is why he gave me three wonderful children to have and hold , look after and be there for them . A lot of people always told me that my children where taking up to much of my time , never going anywhere without them not going out to have a cup of coffee sometimes with my friends , always saying no to any invitations that did not include my kids . They could talk all they liked, for me there was no one more important than my children and that would not change any time soon . My husband knew that too since he was not home much he could see the bond between our children and me was much stronger than the one he had with them but that was because he was very seldom around . Two weeks where over and my baby was supposed to be born any time now but nothing was giving me any indication that it would be soon. Going over the nine months already two weeks , now still nothing . My Doctor who came out to see me told me after an examination that all was well, the baby's heart beat was very strong , telling me that, if in one week there is no pain he will have to start it , you see he said you might have to go in to the Hospital if there is anything that could go wrong you have to go . Having had both of the other children at home this one would be born here too , there would be no way my baby was born in a Hospital besides , you and the Midwife will be here there is nothing that we need otherwise or is there ? No there is not he said but be prepared okay ? Just what I needed, to go to the Hospital , that was one place not to well liked by me for a good reason . Not to worry just yet, the Doctor said it can still be all okay the baby might just need another week to be ready for this world . Believing with all my heart that all would be okay, since God had been listening to me so well , he would not let anything happen to this baby either , after all of the other things we had to go through this would be okay . But the baby needed more than two weeks and still did not make any motions to be coming on his own . It was now ten months since the pregnancy started but the baby did not want to come, so the Midwife came this one afternoon telling me she would have to induce the Labor and so she did ,that same night my third child was born , a boy , we named him , Joerg Ren'e he was beautiful his very black hair and dark brown eyes mad him look as if he had been for a Holiday in Spain or something , my Mother was so happy when she was told over the phone what he looked like . He would not have come on his own , my Doctor told me right after the Midwife brought my baby in for me to hold him , he had the umbilical cord around his neck , that was the reason he would not have been able to come on his own , remembering the Doctor arriving after the Midwife had phoned him, also my Girlfriend was there she had heard the Midwife telling the doctor on the phone he better get over here fast because there was something wrong with the baby . Which in turn made him come right away , he even closed his Practice earlier so he could stay with me if needed to be . As he was telling me that all went well and the baby was healthy you can imagine how happy that made me feel but the thanks went to someone very special to my Heart , God , needless to say my prayer after everybody had left took about an hour , just talking to him did so much for me and the baby . Nobody who has not have that relationship with God or who has forgotten he had one , can feel the way I felt that night , all was forgotten the pain, the thought of loosing the baby in the mid term , now it was nothing but the past and that was a very good thing .

Thinking about my Mother after my husband had phoned her with the news that we had another boy , she was so happy , when phoning her next day she wanted me to come up to see her with the baby . Mom that can not be right now , he is still to small and to young we have to wait at least four to six weeks the doctor told me, besides it is February and winter still outside . Sorry , she said totally forgot about that ,good that you remembered she said, it is nice to find out that some of the things that where thought to you have stuck with you , I am glad for that she said . Oh Mom I would love to come and show him to you and as soon as he is strong enough you will get to see him okay ?That is great now there is something to look forward too she told me , Mom , I love you , I know you do she said , I love you too . Hanging up the phone was hard for me that day thinking about if my Mother would still live to see this new baby of mine grow up ? The doctors had told us that if she got another Heart attack she would not survive that , now the power of a Prayer was needed , God was the only one who could grant me that wish that my Mother would see this new son of mine , it took about twenty minutes to pray but I do believe he had listened to me because I got my wish . As my son was about five and half week old the weather had let up a bit and it got warmer , enough to take him to see my Mom, it was a Wednesday afternoon and having phoned and talked to my Dad , knew that my mom was doing well , he had not told her yet that we where coming . Just hoping it would not be too much for here and that my dad would have told her by the time we reached their House .Because any surprise could cause her to have another attack and that was the least we wanted . The Cab stopped right in front of the House when we got out , that is my Children and I , my husband was somewhere in Belgium on a Job assignment for the past three weeks, he would not be coming home for about two more weeks this time . We where getting used to this already and knew how to cope with his absents . My Mother was so happy to see the new baby , she could not believe how he looked , he looks like my Brother she said , the same little nose the dark Hair and eyes , at least one of your children looks like from our family . She wanted the baby on her bed the whole time, I had to feed him there and change his diapers but she would not let me take him away from her, and giving in to her for me was easy , there was nobody like my Mother she had always been there for me throughout my whole life, if there was anything going on she was always there for me never said she had no time for me or anything like that , never !

    Now this was my turn in letting her have her way , Mom we are going to come back up this weekend if that is okay with you , we need to wash your Windows on the outside okay ? Fine by me she said but the baby will be staying with me when you come back right , of course he will you have my word on that . Claudia my oldest sat on my Moms bed as well while Dieter was going outside with Grandpa , then I could hear Claudia singing to my Mom she could sing this little girl she loved to sing to her Grandma and my Moms face lithe up like a sun ray . It was a very good afternoon and promising her to come back on Saturday was what we did , today being Wednesday that would mean in two days we would be here again . On my way home with the children in the Cab there was a very strange feeling that came over me , it was like someone was telling me something but I did not want to hear it , since the payer about my Mother to stay alive till she could see my new baby was weeks away there was no connection in my feelings towards that day. But that feeling stayed with me, phoning my Mom every day had become a habit but a nice one, after having talked to her the two older Children took their turn each it was such a nice time always. On Friday night getting ready to go up to see my Mom on Saturday morning, I needed to pack some of the Children clothes they always got quite dirty when we stayed up there for the whole day playing outside would do that but that was okay with me, they always had fun with my Dad playing with some of the Animals. After putting the Children to bed that night, the strange feeling came over me again, what is this, now I got nervous this was not like me what could do this to me, sitting down in my Living room not being able to go to bed , a prayer would do the trick for me it always did ," drear God please let tomorrow be a good day for Mom, help her to be strong enough to cope with having us up there, you have heard her, she wanted us to come even if I did not think we should, so short after the Wednesday, please God stay with her and give her strength and let her know how much we all love her. Please do not take her from me just yet ,without her I can not exist, my life would be very dark and I would be lost, you have given me such a great Mom and Dad please let me keep them for a long time to come, in turn you have my word that my children will learn more about you I will always tell them about you and the Bible but please keep my Mom alive for me please. Not noticing that tears had run down my cheeks, sitting there for a while praying but as soon as the prayer was finished, my door bell rang, my Heart stopped for a moment knowing full well what had happened, going to the front window to see who wanted to be let in, my Husband had a key he could not have been the one . Then I could see my Sister standing down there and it hit me right there , while pressing the buzzer to let her in down stairs started to get dressed again, knowing what had happened , my Mother had died , all feeling left my whole body sliding down the wall when my sister came in the door ,she saw me sitting in the Hallway on the Floor. My sister came in she could not get me up it was like all life had left my body . What had just happened , God always listened to me he always gave me my wish , why is he being so mean ? We have to go to the Hospital my sister said can you get Franziska to come down to be with the children , Mom has just died we have to bring her some clothes , did you want to see her one more time ? How could she be so collected , it was like she did not care if my Mother had died , but then she never had a good relationship with my Mom because when both of us had started to work, at the same time , she was left behind in School because she had Scarlet Fever when she was seven . We both graduated the same time out of Grade eight , that was as high as you could go in those days but you started a job right away and once a week had to go to a School , it was like a Gymnasium where we learned all about how to handle Money look after Children and so ,on the boys of course would learn all about having families looking out for them and going to learn some kind of trade . Which we actually did too, except my Sister did not want to learn anything she went to work in a Chemical Factory, where I went in to the Textile Industry . But my Mom caught my sister stealing from her by not giving her the full amount on her pay days , she had done that for two years, so needless to say after that the good relationship they once had was no more , my Mother was very sad about that . Any way still sitting on the floor , not caring what my sister was saying ,crying the whole time she was talking ,what did you just say , looking up at her it was like looking through her . Sure I could hear her but as if through a fogy sky it was like there was an echo when she spoke , "would you like to see Mom one more time , if yes you have to come with me right now we have to bring clothes for her ! She helped me get up from the floor , still shaking like a tree in the wind , my hands could not hold the phone ,so she dialed the number of my Girlfriend who came right away when she heard what had happened . Sure I can sit with the children no problem , turning to my sister I could hear her say , just make sure that you bring her home we can look after her , my Mom is coming at about eight in the morning she can sit with Monika for today . Driving up to the Hospital still thinking it might all be a joke that my sister was playing on me it would not be the first time , she had phoned me one night telling me that my mom had died just to get at me because my Mother had said to her how much help I had been . But walking down this long hallway towards the end where they had my Mother in a room to be getting ready for her open casket . Walking in to that room the whole realization came over me , my Mother would never be there for me ever again, she truly had died but as my Dad told me later that day , she had died very happy knowing that my new baby boy looked so much like her brother who had died four years earlier . Thinking back now it was strange, because all my Moms sisters and her Brother died within four years of each other it was very strange to me indeed . For now the whole world came to an end , my Dad brought me home and stayed with me for a few hours until my Girlfriends mom arrived she was such a lovely Lady . Taking very much comfort in her being with me that day looking after the children which in my condition was not possible , for me there was no tomorrow , my dad just said to me on the way home from the Hospital , are you glad now that we did not tell her about your Husband ? You see , my Husband had been escorted out of the apartment by the Police the Friday after being up at my Parents House to show my mom the new baby , he had beaten me up and friends had phoned my Attorney he in turn had phoned the Police to get him out . In the back of my mind I had always hoped my Mother would recover ,we always had such a good time talking sitting up all hours of the night when either one of us could not sleep but she never found out about my Husband , at the time we had been afraid it might give her another Heart attack , that we did not want . But now she got one any way , walking in to my bath room I started to talk to God again but this time it was not really a prayer , because he had betrayed me very much , at least that was my out look at that time . Saying things like , " today is the last time that you will hear a Prayer come out of this mouth , you have betrayed me very badly , how could you take the most important person away from me , out of my life ? You know very well that my Mother was always there for me she was my back bone my Anchor when it was needed , now you have taken her away after all the prayers that where said to keep her with us for a few more years." Today is the last time that you will hear my prayer since you apparently do not care about me as you have shown me in the past few weeks , now I do not care to talk to you ever again . Whit saying that I felt something pulling at my Heart truly pulling , but when one is so stricken with grief there is no arguing, never listen to my Father who told me that now ,you have to be strong for your children . Why should I do that , since God does not care one way or the other why should that make me listen to anything that my dad was trying to tell me ? From that day on there was no more prayer from my lips , my children where all that mattered to me any more , my friends mom came over a lot to talk to me and in a way it helped very much , but when she asked me to go out with her daughter to go where a lot of people are to get out of this House ,,meanwhile the children and I had moved in to the House we had been building , it was finally finished . Very nice three bedroom house with garden in front and back . Now this would mean a bit more work but it still was not enough for me , phoning some of my old friends from the Textile Factory finally got my old Boss on the line one day asking him if it would be possible to get some work to do at home . The main thing for me was at that time not to leave my children , since my Mom had died I was afraid they might not be there when getting back , which of course is silly but to me it was not . Today knowing that it was just the loss of my mom that made me behave like that it made sense to me but at that time nobody was able to make me change my mind . After my last baby was about two years old one of my brothers came to visit , Helmut , he had a Restaurant and was well known for his roasted chicken , People from all over came to his place to have a taste of that chicken . Today he came to visit me, to say that he was thinking that it would be a good idea for me to come up to his Restaurant with the children and have dinner with him and his Wife , of course if the children can come that is okay with me we will be there . He gave ma a hug which was very unusual for him but he told me that he had the feeling the hug was needed very badly and he was right . Since the loss of my Mother and the split up from my Husband the world had no meaning for me any more only the children where important in my life nothing else . As luck would have it , being at my brothers Restaurant which I had invited my best friend Franziska too as well , one old friend of mine was there that day too , we had grown up together and he knew all about my life, there was nothing anybody did not know about anybody because in a small place that is how it is . My Friend Burghardt came over to where we where sitting , he started talking to me also giving me a big hug , "how are you he asked ? " Well actually very good aside from the weather that we been having life is good ! He looked at me , "than why are your eyes not smiling when your mouth is , what has happened to you to be so cold and sinister looking , what happened to the smiling Girl we all knew , that one with the laugh lines all over her face ?" You always had a smile for everybody , but now that is not there , can I do anything for you , he looked at me , we have been friends for such a long time always ready to help one another so now let it be my turn okay ? That is all well but if you ask me , there is nobody who can help me there is no need for help !

Looking up because my brother was coming to the table bringing dinner for the children , what would you like , looking at me , but my appetite was not very good since the last two years , hardly eat anything at all just had some juice ,not being a drinker of beer or wine it was easy to please me with a lemonade . Out of the corner of my eye there was this shadow coming towards the table , my friend had seated himself for a while but this was a stranger , Burghardt got up to introduce his friend , this is Peter, he said , he is a fellow Army buddy of mine he is going to come with me for a few weeks since he has not been here we thought he might come and get some of your Brothers good chicken . Well the whole trip just for chicken , my voice was dripping with irony , you probably would get good chicken somewhere else as well ! My brother who had overheard me came over asking me to go with him in to the kitchen just for a minute , my Girlfriend was staying with the children ,what is so important that you wanted me to come in here with you for ? Might I say that you are impossible to talk to , he had not spoken in that tone of voice to me ever before , just very surprised by looking at him could see he was very serious about this , if you do that one more time I will come over to your table put you across my knees and give you a good spanking , you need one I can tell , he said ! Don't you dare , why do they have to come and sit with us at our table , nobody called them over besides , if he thinks that I would go out with his friend than he is very much mistaken . Men have no meaning to me any more , remember what the last one did and he was my husband supposedly looking out for my well being, but what did he do ? Not all men are alike my brother said , 'you have to give life another chance mom has been dead for over two years , your divorce has been two years now , you never leave your house , the only once who profit from your kind of life are your children , but there is much more out there . Surly God did not mean for you to live like in seclusion , leave God out of this he does not care about me or my children , there is no way he would care now . Please do not say that , he said , his eyes gotten very dark , please you have to get out of this or you go under , your whole life you have believed in him more than any of us ,now it seems that you do not care on way or the other ! You got that right I said , caring is for people who believe I do not any more after all , God has taken everything that meant anything to me away from me , my whole life he sheltered me kept me save but ever since

Mom died there is a part of me that does not believe any more in his being there for me . Turning around going back in to the Restaurant seeing my children sitting there having their dinner , a bit of a warm glow came over me just looking at them , they had become my life nothing else counts any more but my Children nothing and nobody !

   Sitting down seeing that my friend Burghardt had left whit Peter nodded my head at my Girlfriend to hurry up because the children needed to go to bed and there was some work still waiting for me at home . One thing was great , to have a friend like Franzy how we called her , she and her Mother had been a big help and comfort to me over the past two years always there for me coming to visit looking after the children playing with them , to this day my Children call my Girlfriends Mother , "Oma lustig ". Which means ,Grandma happy , because she was always so full of cheer and good words for all of us never had a bad day, we where so fortunate to have her around . Specially me , whenever a day truly got me down , all   that was needed to do was phone her , she would come as soon as she could just to talk to me . My Father and two brothers came often too but none of my sisters , there where four of them but they believed that I deserved everything that had come my way !May be there right by gully , my life had been very sheltered never had to make a decision on my own , my Mother was always there and then my Husband, going through life as a happy go lucky person it was hard to understand why all of a sudden the whole world came crumbling down on me.

   God could not be that nasty to let me have all kinds of bad things to deal with , but than may be he was , my thoughts where still with that while sitting in the car driving home , hardly heard Franzy say that Burghardt was coming to my house to pick her up and if you like to go with us we love to go out to dance for a little while . When did you decide that , asking her facing the road , my driving left something to be desired always going to fast , but than life did not mean a lot to me at this point and time but when Franzy told me to slow down , you got your children in this car don't you care about there health ? Of course I do ,so sorry , it finally dawned on my that I had better be more careful or my children would be lost to me to. May be my brother was right I needed to smarten up . But why is Burghardt picking you up again , I was not listening very well . He wanted to know if you would like to come too , Peter, his friend is coming with us it would be great getting out for a change right ! When was the last time that we had been out on the town , it was a long time ago, it seemed like ages , it sounded nice to go dancing , but what about my children , do not worry she said , my Mom will be at your house when we get there so all is settled . Bringing my children to bed was always something nobody else would do for me , and funny enough they always had to say their prayer , even if their Mother did not pray any more, but that did not mean they could not , after all it was not their fault that all those bad things happened to me . Arriving at my house Oma was there already with Franzies son Peter, he was eight years old at the time and loved to baby sit my children even if only in present of an adult he did not care at least he could talk to them and play with them . Since his Father had died , he was very lonely, just like my friend but tonight we would go out . After having put the children to bed we got changed it did not take long for the two guys to pick us up . What is your hurry , looking at my girlfriend who motioned me not to be so sarcastic , please Monika , not tonight okay , try to enjoy this night just try !Okay may she was right and it would be the way to do , Burghardt took Franzy's arm while Peter tried to take mine but very abrupt , made sure that he would not do that again, at least not until it was permitted by me for him to do so after all , until tonight I had never seen him nor did that make me like him more or less, so a little distance would be good okay ? He had understood but after all of that it would turn out to be a very nice evening , my friends where great and for once in a long time my smile had come back , I am just great full to the both of you to make me come with you , turning to Peter , my apology to you too , it is just that after all that has happened there is not a lot of trust in me right now, it will take a while . Why don't you just trust in God he knows what he is doing, there must be a reason for me being here tonight with your friend , or may be it is faith . Do not tell me about faith or God for now that is a subject this one will not listen too okay . What has been so bad that you need to speak like this , Peter asked . How much time have you got, a month or two ? May be one day when we get to know each other better we can talk about that , but for now it is something that one has to deal with alone . Peter did not like my answer but he had no choice , after all one can not turn around like that from one minute to another , it took more than two years it will take a bit longer to turn around and trust someone again . Next day my dad was coming to visit when talking to him about the night before he could not believe that his Daughter had behaved so badly , " what is wrong with you , why can't you be nicer to some one ,what had he done to you to deserve that , if you are mad at someone than do not let another person bare the heat of it . Another Man would have hit you do you realize that but he is probably one of the most decent human beings because if he still wants to see you again he must be an Angel . There are no angels remember , not here not anywhere if there would be my life would be different , Mom would still be here !

If you can not accept that your mother is better of where she is now than that is your problem and yours alone , you had looked after her and seen how much she was suffering , how can you have wanted her to live like that just because you are so selfish and wanted her to be there for you . How stupid can you get , Monika , you got to wake up and smell the Roses again , Mom would not have wanted you to be this way , she was always so proud of you because no matter what you could be so happy even in the darkest hour you smiled and said , God knows what he is doing , he will make everything right ! Have you completely forgotten that , why do you think he let you be on your own , you needed to grow up without having Mom by your side to pick you up every time you struggled and fell . Thru she was always there for you no matter what but she always let you make up your own mind remember ? By now it felt like I was sinking again , never had my Dad talked to me this way , how come he is so mad at me , why are you doing this to me , asking him this while tears where running down my cheeks , why , because you have forgotten where you come from , you treat everybody with contempt , needless if they have done anything to you or not , this has got to stop before you turn in to a very bitter Woman !Oh Dad , I do not know any more what to do , Helmut had talked to me about this already so did Harry but now you , it must be my fault and there is only one who can help me but I have not talked to him in over two years may be it is to late ? It is never to late , my Dad said , if you truly want his help now is the time to ask for it , there is no way that you find out of this on your own you have hurt so many people already, even your own children by telling them that God is not always good when you know in your Heart , that all he does is because he loves all of us and he loves you very much , look at your three children , they are the most beautiful kids any one could have but you have not thanked him enough for that . Instead you had to be mad at him for letting you grow up without having Mom there , if she would be here right now you know what she would say right ? May be , but there is so much inside me that has gotten bitter for far too long , you are right , this is the time that things turn around . From that day on that very same night my Prayer was a very long one ," Dear God , hope you are still listening to me , since being mad at you for so long the start is hard for me but you have made my life very hard in the past two years , having my mother die was like you took a piece of my Heart and never gave it back to me . You are the only one who knows how much my Mother meant to me , to this day the hurt is still so bad sometimes that I would like to go to the Graveyard and dig her up, she needed to be here for me and my children . But Dad is right if she needed to be here you would have left her here , she was very ill and the best way was to take her with you . Today I have come to understand what you did , it is good to know that you still care enough to make me see that your ways are always the right once no matter what we want , how could this happen to me to become so dumb not to see that any more . Throughout my whole life you have guided me sheltered me from harm now I have behaved like this ,why is my brain so small as to only see what is important to me and not what you want for me and my children ? How can we ever get back this relationship between us , it made me feel very safe all the time but now there is no safety felling already for a long time , tell me what can be done and it will be on my part any way . Hope that we can talk every day again now since my children are praying to you please listen to my prayers again as well okay ?" After that prayer it began to be a little bit more peaceful around me that same night the Dream I had was about my Mom , she was telling me that she was very proud of me for the way that my children where brought up and the way they looked , always nice and clean she said , but you have to make your self a bit more presentable again my sweetie she said , it is time to let go of me okay , I am fine and have no more pain ,but you have to let go of me now please . Waking up and looking at the clock it was only two in the morning , but getting up and going downstairs was as if someone had told me to do that by walking out of my Room there was a noise coming from my youngest sons room , he had a hard time breathing , what was this , running to his bed I could see that he had a hard time getting air picking him up holding him on my arms going downstairs with him and outside to the back yard was helping him ,but it scared me very much . Is that what is the answer to my prayer , thinking like this had gotten me nowhere but walking back in to the house , phoned the children's specialist whose phone number was right by the kitchen counter , Joerg had breathing problems before but nothing like this , the emergency Nurse told me to get to the Hospital right away with him she would let the doctor know he would meet me there . Having to get the other two children up was not easy but when telling them what was going on they got dressed in a hurry , Claudia was like a little Mother to Joerg , how are you feeling she asked him , just sit very still until Mom can get you to the car okay ? He smiled at her but than started crying , this was not good , it would make his breathing even worst , please Dieter hurry up we have to get your brother to the hospital . Going in to the emergency it was like we had been here yesterday , looking at my Mother , the whole hurt came down on me again but this time there was no way of giving in to that , my son was more important than my stupid selfish pain, it would not do for me to mourn my Mother while my son needed me so badly .Feeling Gods present right at this moment when the Doctor came towards me , taking Joerg out of my arms telling me to sit here and wait with the two other children , we bring him right back we just have to get his breathing to normal okay ? Sitting there feeling totally lost there was this little hand that was feeling his way in to mine on one side but than on the other hand too ,looking down in to two pairs of eyes as blue as the sky , seeing that they where afraid for their little brother made me realize that they needed me much more than anybody else in this world , they depended on me to keep them save to love them and hold them close to my Heart , just what my Mom had always told me . She had always said that children are the most important things in a mothers life they needed us to look after them but not only that , they where gifts that came from Heaven for us to have our happy times with as well as sad but also to keep them safe and give them a lot of love and show them that there is right and wrong . This was my wake up call right here , hearing my moms voice telling me to let go of her but look after my kids better not getting so caught up in self pity, not seeing what is real important in life any more . While holding on to my children's hands asking them to pray with me for their little brother , our old

Family Doctor came along , he noticed us sitting their , coming over asking ," why are you here what happened ,where is Joerg ? He is in with the children's Specialist he had one of his breathing attacks tonight , this is morning already where did he go with him , pointing at the door they had walked through he turned around going in the same direction . What was going on why did they keep my son in there for so long . Well as we found out later they where having him on the Oxygen apparatus because he could not get enough air ,he had said that his Mommy was very upset and he believed that it was because of him , he felt just because he is not very well that would be the reason for me to always cry . It had gotten him in such a state that he could not breathe any more , Monika , the Doctor said , please let me explain to you what you can do to make this go away . If you can get away with the children just for a weekend to the North Sea , they have great cabins in Belgium you could stay there with them for three days , let Joerg run without a jacket just in a T Shirt so the wind can go through him after three days of that he will be much better and you would not have to worry about his problem any more . He does not have Asthma but his Bronchial tubes are too small so when he gets upset that is when they clinch together more and make his breathing very hard . But a good Sea wind will cure him of that . Looking at the Doctor believing that he was not all there upstairs , he noticed my looks , if you do not believe me than give it a try , and when you come back and he has not gotten better I will personally see to it that you and your three children can go on a nice three week holiday okay ? That was not okay of course still not believing that something so simple would make my son better but not dismissing it totally just yet , may be there was something in that , it could easy be that God finally was showing me to trust him again, more than any Doctor more than my own thoughts . Phoning around as soon as we got home made me also phone my brother , this being a Friday morning was not easy to speak to any body most people where at work , a very funny thing occurred , while talking to my Brother who was already in his Restaurant found out that he had two visitors . My childhood friend was there with Peter who had both offered to help my Brother on this day because there was some kind of tournament with the Gaming Machines ,my brother had two of those installed not to long ago and he was expecting about one hundred and twenty people for dinner that Friday night . Telling him exactly what our old Family doctor had told me he was listening ,okay he said , let me think about this for a few minutes and I call you back . Not knowing at that instant that those two guys where there with him, could also not know what would happen next . My Brother did not phone back for about twenty minutes when calling him he only told me that all would be taken care of , the children and you will be in Belgium for about four days you stay in a very nice Cabin all the arrangements have been made just start packing . My voice was fading out my throat felt like it was getting to small to say anything , but when thanking him he said , do not thank me for this,there is someone who cares a great deal about you and the children he will be at your door in a few minutes and take you and the kids to Belgium . What did he just say , that was hard to believe that someone would come to take her and the kids to the Sea , but there is no time to wait around , packing clothes and food was in order she needed to take a lot for four days with three children there is a lot to think about what one needed to take specially for

Joerg. She did pack a Jacket for him as well as some very nice warm sweaters and rubber boots for all three of them since she had all of that any way she might as well take it with her . When the door Bell rang running from upstairs to see who it was she was absolutely surprised by the person who was at her door ! What can I do for you she asked Peter , yes, it was he who was at her door she could not believe this , after being so nasty to him the other week why would he bother to come and help her ? There was no time to figure that out just yet , she had not told the children that they where going away for a few days so she called Claudia Dieter and Joerg inside they had been playing out side in the back yard !

We are going on a trip she told them is there anything that you would like to take to play with while we are there ? Where are we going Mom , Claudia asked ,well we are going to stay in a Cabin by the Seaside in Belgium for a few days because that is what the Doctor had told me to do for Joerg . Peter has come to take us there ,who is he, Claudia wanted to know . He is a friend of a friend from my childhood , and he will bring us there ,but I do not know who is going to pick us up may be we should take our car . No need for that Peter said because not only do I take you there, but also bring you back home . How is that going to work out , looking at him there was a warm feeling , his blue eyes where so clear nothing hidden in them just straight forward looks she got , well he began to explain , your brother believed it would be a good idea for me to stay with all of you and bring you back home after the weekend . How can that be, do you not have to go to Mons to be at your job ,not for another week he said , as Burghardt and me we have two weeks Holiday ,we do not have to be back for another week , there is all the time in the world to bring you back as well . Why would you do that for me the last time remember ,not being to nice to you , just now have to wonder why you are doing this . Well because not only do you mean a lot to me it also means a lot if I can help you in any way you see , since meeting you for the first time you had left a very big impression in my mind , every since then as much as I try can not forget you , what do you think this means , smiling he looked at me , do not get your hopes up, there is no way that I would get involved with another Man , been there done that did not work and the last beating was enough for me to stay away from Men for a long time . His face darkened there for a few seconds , you will never see me even just lifting a hand against any woman specially not you for that matter . Turning around grabbing two of the suitcases sitting in the hallway he walked out the door to his car   , there was just enough time to phone Franzy to tell her what was going on , she was so glad , finally she said , it is just about time that you give Peter the benefit of a doubt he is not like most Men he probably loves you very much at least he cares enough to bring you and the kids to a nice place for a few days . Is he paying for the stay there she wanted to know , oh no , my brother is but he is getting the money back from me as soon as we return . Have a great time and do not think to much about anything just enjoy the time there , he must be Heaven sent because never has anyone done anything like that for me in all the years after my Husband died , Franzy said .Well you might be right , may be God is telling me something and may be my Father is right too when he told me that it is better to forget all the bad things that have happened and start living again for once ,that is a good idea my Friend she said , have a great time get some rest too the house and garden will be looked

after you know that right ? What would I do without you , a Friend like you is nowhere else to be found, thank you and we see you when we get back okay ? Give my love to the children and Moms too , she wanted to come over tonight but that is okay we can do that when you are back . Peter came back inside asking if there would be any more bags or suitcases to carry out to the car , no there aren't all there is to do is to check all water faucets and close all the windows and lock the Door . Said and done sitting in the car close to Peter was not a good feeling to me it was like sitting in the back with the children but there was no room it made me kind of nervous to, sitting so close to a Man that was hardly a friend , but than he wanted to be more than that to be sure ,God what is it going to be , this would have been the last thing that would have been chosen by myself , to be sitting next to Peter . Moving slowly over to the outer corner of the seat right by the door he looked over to me , are you afraid of something , you do not have to be , there is nothing that I want from you if not given freely by you , never would lay a hand on you or the children no matter what you can believe that , God is my witness !

Sorry but it makes me nervous to think that you volunteered to bring me to the cabin may car would have taken us there too , yes but your brother was worried that you might be to emotional right now and not a very safe driver , he wanted to bring you there himself but as you know he has got a very busy evening and needs to be at his Restaurant . And that gave you the edge you needed to get close to me , she wanted to take that back already as soon as it was out , he had done nothing to warrant any of this he was being very nice about all of this ,remembering her Dads words she said , sorry that was uncalled for it won't happen again , promise .

No harm done he said , as a Soldier we are very though so if there are any other frustrations that you like to get of you chest please feel free but do not make me out to be a heavy , my intentions are honorable from the beginning or did I do anything to upset you ? No you did not but the thing is for a long time now it is hard for me to trust any Man not only you but anybody . That is understandable but it would be nice if you could give me just a little benefit of a doubt it would make it easier for us to stay in the same Cabin . My heart set out right there for a few seconds , had he said we stay in the same cabin ? That was not acceptable for me telling him this he said . there was no other way honest we had phoned around and all the places are busy and rented out for this weekend the only cabin we could get was the one with the three bedrooms so the boys can take one of them , Claudia and you can take the other ,while the last one is for myself . Is that okay with you , yes it is but still not the perfect solution we just have to make the best of it . Right now that was all that was to say about that leaning back a bit more relaxed saying a prayer was the only thing to do for me , God if you can hear me , tell me what you want me to do , you know that trust is a very bad word for me right now , trusting you has just come about again after all that time not speaking to you , please you got to help me . Make me feel more at easy with this situation , he is a nice Man and may be , just may be you have send him , than let me know one way or the other please , because the feeling that goes through me right now is that of resentment towards my brother for letting this man Peter take me instead of him ,knowing full well that it is all done with the best intention and my children's well being in mind as mine too .But even after knowing all this dear God , your help is badly needed by me as if you did not know that , please be not mad at me any more for not talking to you for such a long time from now on there will be talks for you and me every day twice or may be three times , Just let me say this ,please let Joerg be okay after this promise me that he will be healthy again you have it in your hands , this trip is all about Joerg not me or Peter or anybody else it is just for my little boy and for him I can live with the knowledge that we have to share a cabin . Thank you for listening please bring us there save and look after our house while we are gone and bring us back save too ,this I pray in Jesus

    Name , Amen !

    You are very quiet all of a sudden Peter said while looking over to where I was sitting , the children where playing with some new toys he had brought for them , the boys got some very nice Match box Cars while Claudia got a brand new Doll , why he did this is beyond me ,but it was nice to hear my children chatter away behind me, once in a while there was a laugh too coming from them , that did my Heart so good , it has been a long time for me to realize that the children had been suffering under my behavior always being so nasty to any outsider ,not to them of course but to every body else for that matter, now it was time to stop all of this and if it was Gods will that we should get together Peter & I so it should be, but for this weekend to be on my Guard was the least that needed to be done . It was only a two hour drive from us to where the Cabin was ,very nice, it had its own kitchen but if one wanted too could go over to the Restaurant to have something to eat , but as always when going on a trip with my children ,would pack a lot of foods they liked also good healthy foods that where good for them . While we where taking in the suitcases, the children asked if they could stay just outside the cabin it was such a lovely warm night , windy , but warm . Just bringing all the things inside that we had packed at home , walking outside to see my children Peter said , why don't we go down to the beach right now just to see how it looks okay ? That was great for all of the kids yes please lets do that , Claudia was taking Peter by the hand and walked right beside him , she had never done that with anybody not even my brother, just Opa and now Peter , what is it that saying , from the mouth of babes , she probably knew that Peter was a good guy , seeing the both of them going right in front of me made my heart feel lighter , it would be nice to be a Family again , even when my Husband was still in the picture he was never home , the children often asked me why we where the only once alone in the playground without their Daddy , how come all the other kids are here with theirs but ours is not here . Many times there was no explanation for that but now seeing them walking with Peter in front of me Joerg had taken Peters other hand Dieter was walking right next to his little brother talking to Peter as if he knew him for a long time already . If only my Mom could be here now she would know what to tell me , she always knew , God , I missed her so much , the old pain started to come back but instead of giving in, fighting it was the better way of dealing with this right there and then because of the children and because promising my Dad that this would be a little holiday for me and the kids. Also promising my girl friend and my self not to do or behave in any way to make my children's faces look sad again . It would turn out to be one of the loveliest evenings that we had in a long time , Claudia was as happy as she had not been in a long time even Joerg who had been so shy when it came to strangers , he was all over Peter throwing sand at him running away from him only to be caught and than lifted up on the shoulders and run around in a circle to make him almost dizzy . For a long time I had not seen my children like this so happy and laughing so much ,God must have his hands in this or this would not be and with that giving in to the happiness was easy for me, for the first time in a long time free from bitterness , promising myself that for the children's sake but also for mine , this would be a great weekend .

It turned out to be one of the greatest weekends we had in a very long time , Peter was a thru Gentlemen never coming to close to me but instead playing with the children running with them going digging for clams or other sea creatures , never a dull moment we all had so much fun, the weekend was over before we knew it . While Joerg had been coughing for the first day on the beach from the second day on there was no more of that, he was running around as if he never had anything wrong with him ever . Most People say it is all in my mind that he was cured that weekend but it is not , having had problems every since he was born and now nothing any more , we could not wait to get back and have our Family Doctor look at him and tell me what had happened . Packing all the kids stuff that we had brought besides the new things Peter had bought them here in that Store it was a sad moment for all of us, for a few days we had forgotten all that had been sad in our life , but promising my children, that from now on we would go out to the open door Swimming Pools if the weather was nice , also every day we would go to any of the many Parks besides that , there needed to be a time with my Dad and showing the children where I used to play when we where small my sister and myself . It had truly changed me, this weekend , nobody could be more surprised than me , never in my wildest dreams would anybody been able to tell me that this would happen, there was no way to believe it unless one was there to experience this . In the Car going home Peter was looking over at me several times until he got the courage to ask me what was on his mind , would you consider going out with me once in a while , the children have told me that would be okay with them , besides we got along so well that the thought has crossed my mind to do this more often, if you can stand being near me . That would not be a problem , but from now on the children will have a better Mother, one who puts them first again as it should have been , not one who is feeling sorry for herself because God has been trying to show her that she could do very well without her Mother being there for her all the time .He has given me a new lease on life to be sure about that , also sending you in to my life must mean something, so yes to your question , if you like we can go out sometimes. Also with the children , let me know ahead of time because from now on that car of mine will be in use a lot ,we have a lot to catch up on . Saying this looking at him and seeing his eyes just like two stars so bright and full of love , but the later was not what was convenient to me right now ,but deep in my Heart could feel that my feeling towards Peter had changed in the past few days . He had been such a good helper with everything, the worries that where in me all that time about Joerg , he knew what to say when to say it , funny how life plays sometimes , specially when we think there is nothing that can make us happy again , there is God . He can show us that even in the darkest hour there can be a light at the end of the day , he makes everything seem like one should not have worried in the first place ,but just let everything happen the way he had planned it . Peter came in to the House with us , asking him if he would like to have a Coffee with me was the least , he knew how much coffee meant to me , for the most part of my life coffee was a big part of it since a small child when drinking a sip from my Moms cup without her knowing it to this day . He was just being polite when he said he was going to love to have some coffee with me because from our mutual friend , who had told me that Peter does not like coffee at all, I knew that he was just going to have some to be with me a bit longer . Not that it offended me in the least , as a matter of fact , my feelings where such that now his company was greatly appreciated to say the least , may be there was more to my feeling than I was willing to admit . But we sat outside , the back yard was nice for the children to play in at the same time we where sheltered form the nosy neighbors while having our coffee . Just wanted to say thank you to you , this was one of the best weekends in my entire Life , truly that is not just saying this , the children where so happy everything was so perfect Joerg is much better now, he has not coughed in days , it was absolutely terrific , you have made this past weekend one that we all will remember for a long time . Perhaps it is not going to be the only one for all of us, he said , taking my hand in to his , you know how I feel about you, there is nothing more to say , only that I can wait until you are ready to have a new relationship , his hand was so gentle he held mine so careful as if worried he might break it . For now all that I can say is this , my feelings towards you have changed in the last two days , when we where on the way home , there was this warm happy feeling when looking at you , right now , it is not what I would like, may be in a few months or even weeks , it will be very different . His smile said it all , I can wait surly ,no hurry, calling the kids to say good by to him, he was still smiling , even when he left , but after he was gone Claudia said , why is Peter not going to stay with us Mom , don't you like him ? Yes ,but it is not that ,he has to go home to where he lives but he is going to be back he told me that he would like to take us on some more trips with him , would you all like that , smiling faces all around , yes oh yes we would like that Mommy all of them came over to me giving me hugs and kisses . Dieter was the most precious one hugging me for the longest time, whispering in to my Ear , love you Mommy but love Uncle Peter too , am glad that he is coming back . Claudia was most happy she had taken to Peter with such a love in her little eyes , she was so sweet , is he going to be our new Daddy she asked , no that he is not , at last not now , we have to get to know him better first don't you think so ,yes Mom . When it was time to go to bed the children where still talking about this past weekend, mind you ,the Beach in Belgium was something to be remembered , there was first about fifty feet of pure beach than there where two areas where the barbed wire was not going to let anybody go through , on the other side the same thing except there where still the remains of bunkers where the Soldiers had been hiding during WW2 . Now to the boys that was a subject all on its own I could hear them talking about that for a long time ,but unlike usual when telling them they needed to go to sleep, this time I did not do that ,let them have their moments it had been a long time for them to become so happy again , as children should be all the time . Now there was for me the realization , about what had been done to them , by me , just because not being able to cope with the loss of my Mother , had made my children just as miserable as myself . From now on no more of that , after going to bed myself finding out that missing Peter right now was a strange feeling to me, how could that be , hardly knowing him was one factor not to feel this way just yet , but on the other hand , where does it say there is no Love at first sight , actually it was not love at first sight but now finding myself missing him very much must mean something . A prayer was always a very good thing for me specially now since talking to God was most important to me again ," Almighty God , if you can hear me ,please listen to my prayer , what is going on with my feelings , by now believing that you have send Peter in to our life is a fact to me , but why this , well you know best, that is a fact too and always has been , you have never done anything to hurt me, never, now that I have realized that please forgive me for being so mad at you . But I do need your help ,please tell me what to do ,keep my children save from any harm , look after Peter too he has been such a good guy the whole weekend , look after my dad , after Harry and Helmut , and also my friend Franzy and her Mother , besides that, after Burghard as well since he was the one who brought Peter in to my life . Thank you God for making Joerg better whatever you do to me or my children from now on is excepted as a fact and the knowledge that you always know best , I love and respect you and all you do for us , thank you very much for bringing us home today and look after Peter bring him home save too , in Jesus Name I pray , Amen ! My Heart felt such a relieve not knowing how to handle that just yet but falling asleep all the same ,this was the first truly good nights sleep that was had by me for a long time , the last thought was about Peter .

Nobody ever told me that Life or Love would be easy , and in my Heart I knew that it would take a long time for me to trust a Man again , no matter how nice he would be , as you have to know ,after my divorce from my Husband finding out that he had another woman who had a child by him , also that he had been sleeping around freely when we where Married made me wonder if any Man could be trusted at all . Having a Father and two brothers who always where there for their Wife and children ,always just working hard being there for their family , that was what I had been hoping for all my life . Never did the thought cross my mind that my Husband would not be like that , having not been listening to so many people who tried to tell me about my first husband what he was doing why he was staying away from home for up to six weeks on end . Always believing him when he told me that he only did that because he loved me and the children and wanted to make a better living for us than he had , growing up . Knowing what kind of childhood he had made it even harder to believe any body else , his father had brought himself a new wife from returning home after the War ,showing his than wife that he would not be living with her and the children any more but instead be with his new found Wife . That was a big mistake as he found out down the road so needless to say he later killed himself , because he could not change the things could not make them right again and his children did not want anything to do with him , that must have been the hardest thing he had to deal with at his age . But knowing all of that I had believed my Husband that he was not sleeping around when confronted with that subject , as a matter of fact , he got really mad at me one time almost hitting me in the face because telling him that it was hard to believe so many people could be lying to me !

Here was the truth staring me right in my face , one day a Postcard arrived at my home it came from Antwerp in Belgium , it was from a Woman who thanked my husband for a lovely weekend , that she was in love with him and her greatest wish was that the baby would look just like him . That same , afternoon , after phoning my dad also phoned the Attorney who was a friend of my father . Telling ,, him what had expired today he asked me to come over to let him see this card and he also had something to tell me . That was one of the darkest days in my, life , because one week after that my Mother died never knowing that the Man she believed to be the right one for me was not . Today, I am glad that she never knew what kind of heel he truly was, but as she always told me , every lie comes out one day and God takes his time to punish the people who think they can do anything they like , they might get away with that for a long time but in the end he is the one who lets them know , this is going to stop right here ! Finding my way back to God was hard since telling him over and over again how much hatred there was in me because of all the things that where lost to me now , but where they really ? Thinking about this one day the realization came like a lightning bolt , the reason my Mother died was because she was very ill , in the sixties and early seventies there was no triple bypass or quadruple bypass , there was nothing that could have saved her unless she should suffer for more than just the three and half years . Also , there was no Medication that could do anything more for her as the one she was already given . Besides , she did not take that medication most at the time never thinking very much about that kind of help ,she was very stubborn about that a. Besides that , loosing her finally made me grow up, stand on my own two feet not relying on my Mother to be there for me all the time , which I had done for twenty two years , right after my Mom died I turned twenty three years old , had three children and worked for the Textile company at night . All that would have not, happened, if, my Mother would have still be alive , as my dad told me , nothing happens without a reason , God always lets us think that we are the once making all the decisions but in truth he is the one , the only way is that he does it so carefully that we believe we are the once making changes . After this weekend with Peter and the children in Belgium there was a need to go to visit my Mother , the children would be staying with my girl friend so that there was a lot of time for me to do what needed to be done, also go see my mom . This was actually the first time visiting her Grave , in almost three years that I could not make myself to go and see her grave ,this would be the day , the reason to go alone was that no matter what or how to cope with this it was God who would be standing beside me . Feeling his presents right next to me looking around if there truly was nobody else, the tears came running like a flood ,in three years crying was not an option for me since trying so hard to be tough for my children but also for my own sanity , nobody ever saw me cry, not even at my moms funeral , the only thing that I remember about that is , my brother Harry was standing right next to me he held on to me because, as they told me later my knees gave out and I was sitting in the dirt . Lucky for me that kneeling down right this day by my Mothers Grave was good , that way nobody would be able to help me get up if falling down again , but nobody needed to, on this day . After ,composing ,,myself don't know how much time had gone by, sitting there ,finally started to talk to my mom . Hi Mom , its me , my voice sounded rough, because still crying and not being able to form the right words , I miss you very much and wish you where still here , not that you need to suffer but healthy and well being the   strong Mother and shoulder that always was there for me , so many times your help would have been needed by me , nobody to talk to but myself , hope you are happy in the new place that you are , please do not forget to come to visit once in a while, just so I know that you are okay , the thought of you not being here to give me a hug or a kiss is sometimes unbearable , by now you must know about my husband ? He was not as nice as you always believed he was , but it is okay , you probably also know that there is a new Man in my life now , well he is not truly in my life yet but it is a beginning , it would be so much easier if you could be here to meet him and tell me that he is okay . There are so many things that need to be said , Claudia misses you very much too she always sings this one song that she used to sing for you , the one about the Oma , when she sings that she looks up to the heaven because she tells me that she is sure that you are up there , by now I believe her too, but there was a time when that was not so . Hope God is good to, you and hopefully not before too long we see each other again . Lots of love from the children , but the person who loves you most and misses you most is sitting right here , on your Grave, or better is kneeling on it . From now on I will be coming more often, having made my peace with God ,he has forgiven me ,that is for sure . To bad to have to go now ,but next time will be soon okay ,this time there will not be three years that have to go by ,but you also know , you are always in my Heart and Dad told me something very nice too the other day when the fear of life had me in its grip , nobody ever truly dies as long as we keep them in our Hearts !

Please stay well , but also don't forget us okay , so that one day ,when we meet again we can get some of those nice hugs and kisses from you once more . The whole time kneeling there was like it was not me that was talking ,but my mothers daughter , to say this in all honesty , there was a fear amongst my family ,specially between my two brothers and my dad that I would kill myself the loss of my mother had been such a shock to me ,to add to that , the way my husband behaved and all the things that came out after that it was too much for me at most times , if not for my children who needed me ,probable sitting here today being able to write about all of this would not be possible for me any more . On my way home I stopped by this very nice Coffee house in which my mom & I always went every Friday afternoon to have a piece of cake and some good coffee , it was the first time too after three years but the owner still recognized me , how are you , we where so sorry to hear about your Mother, she was such a lovely woman . What would you , like , we haven't seen you in ages , how are your children ,how is your Father ? Well my family is doing well , my children are growing up as they say Claudia is now five almost six , pretty soon she will start School , my Father is well too he comes to my house often ,may be on Friday we come in here after going to the Cemetery . That would be great, we love to see you all again , now what can we get for you today , just some pieces of cake to take home my kids are waiting for me and my friend is there with them so we need six pieces make it some different ,kinds you remember the once my, Mom and I used to eat . She was looking at me kind of strange , you still miss your mother terrible aren't you ? Yes , we all do , she did not have to die if there where better Doctors to help her . Sorry , that was not called for , but sometimes the bitter truth is that she was too young to have died already . We know she said , but life goes on , does it not ? Only nodding my head because my voice went again because trying hard not to cry does that to me , but there had been enough crying for one day so this is it . Paying for my cake the lady, said , we only charge you for three pieces the rest we like to give for the children okay ? That is very nice of you thank you , not at all she said , we love to see you and it is good to see that you are looking so good and we hope from now on to see you again .That you will , probably more than you would like ,she smiled , that can't be often enough for us , when you came here with your Mother all the time we always said that it is so nice to see Mother and Daughter being so close not to many Mothers can say that about their child . My Mother was special to say the least it was not hard for me to love her, she was my world until I had children of my own , but still, she was my rock, my shelter, and my biggest love of my life . We, heard about that from some of your friends and we know how much you loved her but God is looking after her now , she gave me a very, short look because she must have known that God was not a subject for me for a long time . Any, way we ,will see you soon , we hope , say hello to your father form us and your Children too okay ? Sure , will, do, thank you again for this cake we are glad that there is a place like yours around my mother always said that you are the best baker around . With that turning towards the door there was a lady coming in who knew my mother too , she was going to start asking me questions about her but telling her that there was no time now to discuss my Mother with her right now went out the door and left her standing there . Not to be rude or anything but for today there would be no more talk about my Mother , my eyes where bright red already enough and it was time to get home anyway .When my children saw me get out of the car holding this cake box the came running to greet me as soon as Franzy had opened the door for them , Mommy is that cake you got there , " yes but we have to get inside first and you have to wash your hands and look nice to be able to get a piece of this okay ? That was the word , piece of cake and they could not get in to the bathroom fast enough , nearly being inside when they where sitting at the kitchen table waiting for the cake . Joerg was doing so well , this afternoon about four we needed to go to see our old Family doctor , wonder what he would make of this , but knowing the answer to that already , he was the one who told me to take Joerg to the seaside in Belgium , now we would find out today , but by my own experience , he was doing so well he has not coughed once since we got home neither did he there for the last two days that we where there .. My friend was so happy to hear about my weekend , this is so great , she said , may be we can all go out together one more time or may be more often ? Nobody knows what the future might bring , saying this to my friend was all for right now , not knowing if Peter was the right one for me and not wanting to know just yet , there needed more time to go by where we could get together with the children . Most of that time was dependent on my children , if they got along with him , he with them , than may be it was okay if we would move in like he had suggested this past weekend . But most of all , he wanted me out of this Town, since he knew my ex was still around and he had heard from Burghardt that he still was a threat to me and the kids , he wanted me to move in with him , but he lived in Belgium , he was a Soldier and an Engineer for the German Army , working in Nato Head Quarters . Why he crossed my path at this time , nobody could tell me, but God knew, that was for sure because Peter kept coming back almost every weekend , he would not bother to phone any more since most times when he had done that , he was told not to come for a visit . He never gave up and it was his, persistence,   and the feeling that he truly loved me , that made him so lovable after a while , he never asked for anything just wanted to be there for the kids and myself . After three months of that , there was a change in me that told me that he would be the right one for me , any Man who can behave like he did with all the rejections that he had to endure by me could not be bad . Never in my life had there been anyone like he was , besides , the children loved him , but may be I would too if being a child , he always brought presents with him for them   , things they loved to have which they would not get from me . Growing up, believing that children should not be spoiled trying not to do that to my children , needless to say they did get some toys but not all they wanted . One Saturday the door bell rang again and in front was Peter , my friend Franzy was there we had a nice chat about having gone to the outdoors Swimming Pool with our, children , she had brought her little boy Peter too, our kids got along so well it was nice , specially since she lost her husband almost at the same time that mine got lost as well . The only difference was , her husband died mine only in my mind because of all the things he did to me , I had to tell everybody that he had died the only once who knew that he did not where my kids and my Father and brothers even my sisters knew , but they never came and there was no knowing how they felt about it unless the time when they told me that I deserved this kind of life . That was nice to hear from them but like my father always had told me , do not listen to any of your sisters they have no idea what they are talking about and all of them are so busy with themselves that they have no space in their brains to listen to any body who has problems . Hearing this from my dad felt actually very good , because my four sisters had never been nice to me in all my life , all the things they had done to me when my Mother or father had not been around , it was no small wonder that the relationship between them and myself was next to nothing even to this day . But not because my forgiving them was not there , it was a long time ago , they had all been forgiven for all the things, but there was no love feeling from my side towards any one of them nothing they could have been strangers for all I cared . Having Peter in the house now was funny besides my dad or my brothers there had not been a Man in this house for a long time but this was the weekend   it was nice that he was there , he was very honest and lovable , not only that , but also in character and that he was , besides that one could feel the love that he had for all of us not just for me but also for the children and it was not a put on but honestly and truly . Franzy was going to go home as soon as Peter had arrived but telling her that she should stay, there was no need for her to go home now, finally convinced her to stay , later my childhood friend would come over and we could have a nice time . Having said that she said that her Mother would come over to my house to sit with the children and we could go out , you have not been out since the first time we went the four of us , please go with us this time , well okay , but not to late, the kids wanted to go to the Park tomorrow you know the new one , the Adventure park , they had been asking about that the past few weeks , and now we like to take them there . Going out was still a problem for me somehow , because my Ex could be out there somewhere ,making problems for us ,or he would come to the house and take the children away , like he had threatened so many times , and never give them back to me . Voicing my worries to them , Peter had been listening , why do you not tell your brother or father to come and sit with the kids , they told you they would, but up to now you have never asked them , please phone any one of them and see what they say . Naturally my dad was the first one to phone and to my surprise he told me that he would be at my house in a short time . Staying over at my house for my dad was not in , since he still had the animals to look after and the dog to feed early in the morning, he did not want to stay over but he told us that we did not have to hurry home , just have some fun he whispered to me as he was going by me , when opening the door for him . Have some fun and do not worry about the kids , nobody is going to come in to this house , promise ! Knowing that he would be with my children made it easier for me to go out , it had been a long time but the fear of running in to my ex was so great that staying home was always the best solution for me . Now with my father here we could get ready for our night on the town , when Burghardt came he told us that he had a great idea , why don't we go to the next town , they have a great disco there, very nice and not to loud, also your ex won't be there he mostly goes to this one here in town , what do you say ? May be that is a good idea , looking at my Father he nodded his head , why did we not think of that sooner , going out somewhere where there is no danger of him being there ,this is just perfect you can relax and enjoy your self . Only God knew how much fear there still was in me, but keeping a brave face , told them okay , we do that , but not too late my dad wants to go home , so we have to be here not all to late please . Peter was the one who assured me that we would not be too late, he knew how much fear there still was within me , not that I needed to tell him , in time we found out that only one of us had to feel something the other one would feel the same thing . This was a great evening almost forgotten by me ,how much fun it could be just to let the guards down and enjoy the time one had , dancing was one of my favorites but sad to say , Peter was not a good dancer but he wanted to talk to me most at the time anyway, so we hardly where dancing .He wanted to know if it would be okay for him to rent a bigger house in Belgium ,because the children and you should come with me and away from here , your house can be rented out , that way you have an income and do not need to go to work . Besides that , there is no need to make money from your side , my pay is enough for all of us plus I like to marry you one of these days , okay for now it is a bit early to talk about this but the love for you and the kids is very great in me, please think about this and do not say no right away ! Well there would be no way to say no , by now my feelings for him where such that , if he would not be in our life he would be greatly missed not only by my children , telling him this made his face turn first very white than red , can you please repeat what you just said , looking at me as if he had not heard what he did . You heard okay , the time we spend together has shown me that you could be the right one for me but there is still some time needed to get to know one another a bit more , if that is okay with you, this much I can tell you now , Love is what is in my heart when thinking of you ,and not only because you are great with my children , you have been very helpful to us, been very patient with me over these Months, how many ,about six , when falling in love with you I could not say but the other day when you phoned , hearing your voice on the phone made my Heart jump and that is when knowing that loving you may be the best thing for me right now . He pressed my hand so hard it almost broke , can we go outside for a moment , okay but why , you will see when we get there , walking outside with him the strangest feeling of being safe from now on came over me , looking up to the sky saying my thank you to God the almighty was the least that one could do at this moment , Peter had gotten a hold of my arm turning me towards him holding me kissing me it felt like this must be heaven , truly , never had a feeling like this come over me , never, not even with my husband, it was always a save and content one but nothing like this . Now this must be the thru love that was going through my mind, while he was still holding me , his face right above mine he was telling me that he had been wanting to do this for a long time he had always known that we belonged together ,but never wanted to pressure me in to anything . When you told me about your feeling a few minutes ago he said , it was like Heaven opened its doors and let me take a look inside , do you know how much I love you ,you will never know for sure ,but we have a life time in which I can show you just how much you mean to me and how much love there is in me for you and the children !

We have to go back inside or Franzy will get worried you remember what she said , every time she does not see me she is very scared for me , lets go back inside and tell the both of them what we had decided okay ? Lets do that , all of a sudden he was so cheerful so happy , the worried eyebrows where now in line where they should have been , funny that one noticed such things when one is in love ,but this must be the best thing that could happen to me and again one more prayer , silent of course , went out and up to the Heavens . Dear God how can I ever thank you for this Man , my dad had told me that he might be heaven send and now that must be thru , thank you and please keep him safe do not take him away from me as soon as my love is given to him , I beg you please let him be with us for as long as we can have him okay ? My prayer went ,on , until Peter nudged me in the side , are you with us , we wanted to tell these guys something and it would be nice if you could say your part as well . Yes so sorry , my thoughts where somewhere else but now to say this much , looking at my girl friend , we have to let you know that we will stay together and be a couple for now only, without being married ,but Peter has asked me that he would like to marry me soon , there are some things we need to do first but for now we are a couple . What do you say to that , she did not say anything but gave me a big hug , finally it worked, thank God , you fallen in love again, by your face I can see that you are truly happy and we both wish you two all the best life has to offer . One thing I do know she said , your Dad will be so happy for you he told me the other day that he wished you and Peter would get together and he got his wish , boy he will be so glad . Nobody can ever say that there are no Angels , mostly people who have the most to be ashamed of will tell you , that they are the best people around ,we had that in my Family , but neither was I an angel never have been , probably would be up in have if being an Angel , but if this was Gods way of telling me , this is to make up for all the hurt for all that you had to endure , than he was the most gracious God there was , because the love between me and Peter was very special , we had the same dreams and that was literally , one morning we woke both up very early because we had dreamed that my ex had come and taken the children and was going to kill the both of us, when starting to tell him what my dream had been about ,he finished it without me having to go on telling him . Those kind of things happened to us often, more and more so that was when we knew , God had send Peter to be with me, as he had intended for me to be with him . Moving to Belgium was hard for me because it meant leaving my Dad behind , my best friend Franzy , her Mom and my two brothers, but lucky for me , we only where two hour drive away from my home town and Peter being the Man he had told me that , any time you get homesick you get in the car and go home okay , just let me know when, so that there is no worry on my part . He was great and after a few weeks he proposed to me officially , naturally I said yes , there was no other Man that would be suited for me to spend the rest of my life with , he was the one and only and God willing we would live happily ever after . But God also had some more stones placed in my way to happiness , he was going to make sure that our love would withstand a lot of turbulence , he just needed to make sure I guess that it was thru love what I was feeling because the time after my move to Belgium was one that should prove to be more maddening than any other time . For the first few months we where nothing but very happy, all of us , the children where going to a kinder garden , they learned how to speak French , Claudia went to a German speaking School , she was happy , but then one day my girlfriend phoned me from Germany , Monika please be careful when you go out , your ex has been at my house he wanted to know where you had moved to but I did not tell him, so he told me that he would go to one of your sisters . Phone your dad to alert him about this ,she said , okay , right away , since the children where still in school and kinder garden , Peter still in his Office, sitting down by the phone my hand was shaking , what is going on, now what does he want from me , we have been divorced for some time what does he want from me ? My Dad answered the phone on the other end , hi dad that was all that came out of my mouth, when he told me that my ex had been at his house , but not to talk to my dad , but my sister who lives upstairs in my dads house . You can imagine the fear that came back ,like the last few years had not existed , that old fear was there again , what did she tell him , asking my dad this was actually a farce, because in my heart knowing my sister had always hated me ,she was not happy with her husband , he was a Drunk and he beat her and her children ,one time when visiting my dad I got right in the middle of one of their fights, when he slapped my sister and then hit his two year old little girl, just because she was afraid of the big Bathtub , that she had never been inside of before, he took the naked baby and hit her several times on the back , at that moment

my brain set out ,seeing the little one been beaten by this stupid Drunk I went in between , with a kettle full of hot water and dumped it all over him , after that I phoned the child services who came to take the children away for five months, until he had gone to a Alcohol help center . So, it was clear to me if my ex had been at her house ,she would have gladly told him where to find me since she was the one who told me that every thing I got was deserved by me . The answer my dad gave me was exactly what my worries had been , clearly she had told him about Peter and that we had moved in with him, also that we would get Married in four weeks . My ex had told me one time right before the divorce that if he could not have me any more, nobody else would be either , now my worst fears had come through , he knew where the children where and that we all lived here with Peter . He would not let it go with that , my feeling told me so , my gut feeling that is, always was able to count on my gut feeling if good or bad news I would know . Any way after hanging up the phone , my dad had alerted my two brothers of the situation , not known to me, one of them was on his way here , my brother Helmut was coming , he was the only one who could get away that fast , he also knew a lot about my ex, he knew enough not to let him get away with anything any more . Meanwhile trying to phone Peter was no use he had told me that they would have meetings all day and was hard to get a hold of , but if needed to be, phone one of his co workers, who than would come to help out with what ever we needed help with . But that was okay we had been talking to our Landlord he lived two houses down from us, he also had told me that if needed help to phone him , he was closer than anybody else , may be he could come and stay here for a while at least until Peter got home. The Kinder Garden and school had been informed not to let anyone take any of the children, only Monika or Peter where the authorities ,who would be permitted to pick them up . Not that my ex knew where the children where ,not even my Dad was told which School or other place they had been in . There was no way for my ex finding out about the children's whereabouts . Now that our Landlord was on his way, my feeling of being all alone subsided , he was here in no time since Peter had told him everything when we first had moved in, he was fully aware that my ex would be trouble, so he had alerted the Police . Let me tell you about he Belgium Police , they never took long to arrive when there was any danger, as a matter of fact they put high priority on the Nato People whoever it might have been . Lucky for me ,because hearing a car drive in to the back of the house where we had the car park , I first believed it was Peter or the Landlord , looking through the window in the kitchen which was also to the back it was neither one of them, but my Ex !

He got out of the car and had seen me looking out , knocking on the back door, he wanted me to let him in , but this time there was no way that the door would be opened to him, he knew that, so, he just grabbed a rock and broke the back window, putting his hand through the opening, wanting to open the door from the inside , I did not wait till he was inside, but ran to the front of the house, opened the front door and ran out . Just at that time the Landlord was coming down the sidewalk , what has happened he asked me , my ex is in the house he broke the back window and is now inside, because there was no way that I would have opened the door for him . Than we both heard someone running through the house coming to the front, since the front door was open ,he knew that it had been my way out . Standing right in front of us ,we heard the Siren from the Police car coming down the road ,but my ex did not know that the Police was coming to our aid, and preceded to attack me and the Landlord pushing me out of the way, to get to the Guy first as he said . Just at that time the Police arrived , he was handcuffed and put in to one of the Patrol cars . Shaking like a leave may be even worst , one Policeman guided me back to the inside of the House , who broke the window he asked in English ,,well my ex did because I would not open the door for him, he took that rock pointing at the rock inside the kitchen , he broke the window with that . He was than brought to one of the Police stations, from there they escorted him to the Belgium -German border from where he was banned to ever enter Belgium again . Nobody knew , at that time that all the borders would be open in years to come, but lucky for us , by then we had made our way to Canada . But for now we needed to think about moving and telling nobody where we are going not even my Father ,even if he was not the one who told my ex, but my sister still lived in the same House , she could find out any way . Now that we knew he would not give up we could brace ourselves against his attacks ,the Police came just in time ,but the best thing for me was that our Landlord had come right away , as if God had told him to hurry , he was there . A lot of things do depend on God , during the past three years I had so many conflicts with him about all the things that would go wrong and had gone wrong in my life , about that all I ever wanted was a whole Family with children, who would be able to enjoy life ,but not be afraid of it . Many other things too ,but now having had to go through all of that , know better , if we have to go through a lot of turbulence and pain and loss of someone ,it is always for the better or to get the better out of us , since my Mother had died not speaking to him for about two years was not right, he had only done what was best for her, not for me , and that was exactly what I had asked him for , to do the best for my Mom , sure I wanted to keep her , but he did not want her to suffer any more than she already had . Knowing that , she had gone through a lot during the War , loosing three of her children , than loosing her Father and Mother it was not easy for here, she had suffered much more than any of us ever will ,in all our life . She never gave up ,and she put up a good fight when she was ill , as she always told me , never to give up, as long as you can do something about those things, do it she had said , do not fall in to the habit of feeling sorry for your self, nobody would appreciate that and in the end it will only be you ,who is standing in front of God the almighty and has to answer to all he is going to ask you . Make up your own mind, do not let others do that for you, it won't pay in the end , besides, some people would rather send you on a wild Goose chase than truly help you . Go by your gut feeling , God gave us all that ability but most People do not use the gifts they got from him , try to find out what makes you happy , what are your strong points , what would you like to do for the rest of your life or after your children leave home and start their own Family ? Most of all ,never even think about throwing your own life away , that is the greatest gift God gave all of us , our life , he gave that with no promise that we would not have pain or suffering in it , but he also made us a promise , 'when you need help with anything, go to sit down somewhere quiet, start to talk to God, ask him what you should do , tell him that you can not do all the things on your own , ask for his help, but ask with your whole Heart , and mean it when you talk to him .In no time you will find out ,that all is much easier than it was in the beginning, and your burden has become much lighter, than when it started . All of that is the will of God , he will help you any time, no matter where you are, always remember , he is there for you when nobody else is , he can bring light in to your darkness how much or how less you need , he knows best . Never be mad at him , because , besides your life, he gave you as the greatest gift, he also gave you some other once , the smile that you can give freely , the humor that you have, the happy go lucky nature that you display , which make people like you so much , once a Lady told me about you she said , you know Kaethe , if you look at your youngest daughter what do you see , well I see a lot of smiling , eyes that sparkle all the time , she seemed to be a happy child , also she brings sunshine in to our life . That is thru she said but you know what the best thing is about her , every time she comes over to our house and we are a bit down she always makes us laugh , and she knows how to get us to smile, it never fails , , but that is one of the greatest gifts any one could have . Now you know what you have to do , and please do not be so sad about mine not being with you after, because , in your Heart I will always be ,no matter where you move to ,or where you go, that is a promise . My Mother was right, she was in my Heart all the time, but sad times still creep up on me on Mothers day , or Christmas , those are the times when she is missed the most, for one or two days the tears flow freely, just because I miss her so much , she also had told me one time that the hurt gets less, but it never goes away , she was right about that too . When Peter got home after work , the people where there repairing the kitchen window , he did not know what had happen , the co worker at his office had left before telling him about my phone call ,so he came home and after telling him who was here and did this he got truly very upset , so much so that I was afraid he would go and do something to my ex ,but he did not, he told me that we have to move away from here all together ,but he did not tell me that he had Canada in mind . For the weekend we had planned to see my, Dad ,we would pick him up at his house but would not stay there but go to my oldest Brothers house . While we where still talking ,my Brother Helmut came in to the house, we had not noticed him at all ,but the children had been playing in the back yard and told him that he should just go inside . Has he been here already , he asked ,yes he has , telling him about that afternoon he said , when dad had phoned me there was nothing more important as to get in to my car and come here ,but there was a long line up at the border and now I missed him , hoping he would still be here, he would have been in for a big surprise , believe me . It is nice to see you , telling him that it is much better this way , the thought of any one of you going to Jail because of him is not what is needed , he will be dealt with severely, specially now that the Belgium Police has brought him over the border, he won't be permitted to come back here ever , and that is a very good thing . Can you stay for Supper , Peter asked him , oh yes , may be you have an extra bed for me tonight so than I would leave in the morning , if that is okay with you ! Sure it is, saying this was easy, because if anyone knew how much appreciation there was in me for Peter now being here, my brother too, the children where save , it could not be better . After supper we where sitting outside, it was such a nice evening and now since we did not have to fear my ex any more, we started talking about the future , our Wedding was in two weeks from today we needed to make plans where we would move too because Peters time in Belgium at Nato would be over . Actually the real name of the place where he was working was called "Shape ," Supreme –Headquarters –Allied –Powers Europe ". He had been here four years , now they would pay his move to anywhere in the world, he could move to where ever he liked and he liked to go to Canada . For me and the children that would mean to go away from my Father ,their Grandfather , also their cousins , Uncles and so on, for them ,even if they are very young , but they would miss a lot of things so would I , there was no guarantee that Peter would have a job or get one ,we did not know anybody there , neither did we have a House or Apartment as of yet . How Peter was looking, at, this we, did, not ,know but he was right about one thing , if we stayed in Germany or any where in Europe , my ex would never give us any piece, as we had just seen today , it could have been a very different outcome if not for the help of People around us and the fact that the children where at school . There was so much to talk about , my brother Helmut was telling me that , if you do not like it there at all you can always come back home and we figure out something else but this way it would be better for all of you ,saver to say the least . Let me think about, this , turning to Peter he nodded , okay but not to long we have to let my Boss know where we would like to move too they have to notify the Mover so they can get their Trucks ready , remember we are not the only once who are leaving here there are about forty soldiers who are going back home . The thought of having to go so far away was very scary to me , the children where happy about it since my brother told them about the Bears and Wolf's , also the Coyotes or the Bobcat ,and so on , the best one was about he Bears , the children wanted to know if we could go and see one of those , well we might but it is still some time till we could do that okay . Dieter and Joerg of course being boys they would like to leave tomorrow , with Claudia the whole idea did not sit very well ,she wanted to stay close to her father, but of course that would never be ,since the whole and sole custody was given to me, their Mother , my ex had all rights towards the children taken away from him because of his behavior . Any way, we only had time now to think about the wedding , Helmut would come he might bring my Dad with him , Harry my oldest Brother had to work that weekend , he could not come ,but we would go see him three weeks after the wedding any way , that was the day we would leave Belgium for good , actually it was quite nice here they had a lot of very nice Parks where we would go, almost twice a week , the children loved it there so much also they had very nice People who loved children , everywhere the kids would get some goodies form someone it was nice and it felt save to a point , but after that day with my ex coming there   the save feeling was gone completely and Peter was right we needed to go far enough away for him to leave us alone . It was a hard decision for the two of us , the boys where all for it ,and Claudia too now that the time came near where we would leave this house and go to Germany , we would stay with Helmut and his wife until the day of our Journey , it was the twenty fourth of April , 1975 that was our departure day . Whit a heavy heart we packed   up all the things we got for our wedding and some of the once that came from my first home the children had a lot of things so there was a whole container that would be shipped overseas . The   destination, was Calgary in the Province of Alberta , we did not even have a Hotel booked since we did not know any   one there   who could tell us which one would be good for us but we did not worry about that too much the worst part was leaving my Father and brothers behind, it was so hard it took another piece of my heart away , by that time I believed that half of my heart was gone already . Now to go and say good by to, Peters, Parents , he did not have such a hard time , he had never been very close to his Parents or his other siblings but it was still hard on all of us . Two days after we where on the way to the Airport , the children where very excited never having been on a Plain was doing that to them , for myself , well the fear and the hurt out weight the excitement   by far, mostly the hurt , Helmut came to the Airport with us but he did not stay , it is to hard for me to see you go, anyway, please lets say our good bys here okay , that was fine with me, but when he gave me his big hug I was hoping he would never let go and keep me there , deep down in my Heart I did not want to go, but looking at my children and at Peter, for all of us to be safer over there than here made it bearable for me to get on the Plain for Canada. Flying time was more than fifteen hours we had to stop over in London from there it would be Toronto Canada and then the last flight destination was Calgary, Alberta. How nice or not so nice it would be, did not matter, right now we just wanted to get away from here at least for a while, in the Air Plain Peter told me that he had left the back door open for us, meaning that if we wanted to come back he would have a job in the Army again, they had offered him another position if he would come back, that was good news, now it was not so final any more and took a bit of the pressure of the both of us. We had a lot of time to think, holding hands gave us the security of having someone to hold on too, also holding hands with the children they would switch seats now and then just so they all could have a turn sitting by the window. All of us where quite tired, the wedding than the moving we had no rest what so ever now it all came out, Claudia fell asleep very quickly than Joerg and Dieter too. For myself it was too much that needed to be figured out, there was no time to sleep that would be done when we got there. Thinking about my Mother again and what she had told me, that there is always a reason for everything that happens, but even if we do not know it, just lets wait and see she said, God always sends us somewhere and we do not have any idea what we are doing there, or what we should do there, but believe me she had said to me so many times, there is a reason for everything and no matter what anybody tells you do not believe it, just believe your Heart and most of all believe in God. Right now that was just what needed to be done, believe, but how could I do that when everything that was loved by me was gone out of my life , there would be no more going to the Coffee house with my Mother now ,nor with my Dad ,not to mention my Brothers who where so far away from me now . Would Peter change now that we have gone so far away , he was the one who wanted to go here so badly , was the real reason another one than he was telling me ? So many question where running through my mind , not knowing what to expect when we got to our destination , how would Calgary be for us , we had never lived in a big City like that always outside the city limits ,my whole life was spend learning doing , working, but what would it be now . Is there a possibility to get a good job for Peter, after all, Engineers are wanted in most places, but in his field we did not know ,what about my profession , there was no textile industry in Calgary we had already acquired about that from my Brothers house at the Emigration Office ,now what would I be doing when we are there . How would the chances for my children be ,what kind of Schools would there be for them ? Nobody could give me an answer ,only God could , he was very quiet right now he did not let me know to much about our new home , it was like my Mother was flying with me here ,she was on my mind the whole time thinking of her words and wondering what she would be doing but than also remembered what she had told me about her biggest move . She did not go on her own free will she was made to go by the Russian Army , but for her it was harder because she lost three children on the way, she had lost her Father she did not know where her Mother was because so many Families where split up during the war , neither could she take anything with her form her home , no clothes only what they all where wearing at the time . What was this then for me , if holding against the things my Mother had to endure on her way to a strange Land which she did no nothing about , sure she could still speak her own language which we won't be able to do , the Land we are going to there is English spoken there ,but none of us except Peter can speak that . Sure the children speak a little bit of French so do I but that is about it , no English when we needed to learn this in School I never paid to much attention to that subject , but also never knew that I would be going to a Country where this Language was spoken . We where landing in Toronto , Peter asked me to get the Passports out and the Emigration Papers for all of us , why , because we are going to go through the Emigration Office in the Airport here before going on to Calgary this is the main Office and we have to go there as soon as we get out of the plain ,what about the suitcases ,they will be going on to Calgary we do not have to pick them up here , they will be put on the plain to Calgary . Still skeptic about that but believing that he does no best got all the papers out holding them in my hand while Joerg was holding on to my left hand and Claudia & Dieter where going in front of us with Peter . The Officers from the Emigration department where not to friendly , but they asked us if we would like to stay in Winnipeg instead of going to Calgary , what does that look like this Winnipeg ? Well it is not like Calgary , here there are no Mountains only flat Prairie where in Alberta you have not only that but the Rockies as well . Peter did not even let me answer , instead he said , we are going to Calgary , we have a job there and a House , but that was a lie we did not have a house nor did we have a job there , so whey was he saying this . Finding out that he had not told them the truth because he did not want to stay there ,but go to our first picked destination which we liked from the pictures only but never the less , we liked the fact that only one hour drive from Calgary there where the Rocky Mountains, which we could go and see any time we wanted to , we both love that also there was a Town called Banff we would love to go and see, we had heard a lot about that too . Now we are sitting in the last plain , still talking to my Mother quiet of course but Peter could tell that this little camper was not to happy , Mom would know what to say , she would know what to do she was such a strong Woman in her days always knowing the right thing to say even if she did not like something but she would make the best of it , just now it felt like she was telling me to smarten up and stop feeling sorry for myself , get your act together and look at your children don't let them down . If she would have sat beside me that was the feeling it gave me , very strong and may be she was sitting there, who knows but she was right , how could I go on thinking about all the negative when we haven't even got there to see what it would be like ,from now on it would be nothing like that any more but positive thinking no matter what happened . One thing that needed to be learned by me was something my Mother always told me while growing up ,since having had four sisters there was a lot that they did or said to me which made me almost hate them at one time or another , there where bad words falling between us , as the youngest I got beat up a lot by all four of them ,not at the same time, but alternating , after a while one was to believe that it was deserved because they said so but the feeling of hatred was there it did not go away and some prayers of mine had the wish for them to be dead it truly had . Telling my Mother about that one time she was sitting with me outside in the Garden peeling Potatoes , why do you hate them she asked , when telling her what they had done to me while she was at her sisters place with my dad she was very upset , why did you not tell me sooner she said , because they told me that ,telling you would result in more abuse by them towards me so there was no point of telling you was there ? May be not but ,one thing you have to remember , you asking God to punish your sisters is not going to fix it , God knows what they are doing and in his own good time will deal with each one of them , that may be so but he is sure taking a long time , saying that as a young girl is excusable but later in life it was another story . You see not only did I ask God to punish them but also to let them die asking him that I rather have no sisters than the once he gave me and for the longest time that was in my prayers every day . After a few years doing just what my Mother had told me , to ignore the abuse they would bestow on me and laugh it of , it was not working so one day I decided that now was my turn , having had my eighteenth birthday feeling grown up and fit enough to stand up to all of them my oldest sister was the first one who found out that it would not be so easy any more to abuse me every time she felt like it , may it be with words or hitting me she would not get away with it any more . Confronting her with that news she was standing in my Mothers kitchen as she turned around slowly to hit me one more time she had a big surprise coming to her , just as she lifted her arm and her hand came close to my face grabbing her by her wrist and turning her arm to her back she called out to my mom . Now listen up , speaking very slowly telling her that there never would be another hit by her in to my face , this is the last time you ever try , if you do again you will find out that this person here in front of you has a lot of hatred towards you in her heart and she will strike back . My Mom was just walking in to the room when she heard the last words , she just looked at me but did not say anything , just looked very sad . But what is wrong Mom asking her after my sister had left the room , well you know she said , today you stepped down to your sisters level and yet you had so much potential ,not to do that but now it has happened , not that I blame you for it , no ,but God is not having a good day with you today , if you continue to do this to the other sisters you will be just like they are don't you see . Right now you are a much better Person than all four together but if you behave like they do you are no better . But Mom all I did was not to take any more of Erika 's abuse she was going to hit me again and just grabbing her arm to fend her of was not a bad idea was it ? Not really , but just leave God to do his work , and you do the one he has given to you okay ? From that time on I never confronted any of my sisters again as a matter of fact, they could say or do what ever they liked , there was no response from me ,just a smile or a shrug of my shoulders, but that was it, mostly walking away from it was the best thing to do . But one day , after my Mother had died I finally found out why my sisters all behaved that way toward me , when we all went to the House after the funeral they started talking about my Mom and how she always helped anybody , that was the reason why there had been so many People at her funeral , all the once she helped had come to say good by to her . Most of all , they where talking about all the things they had to do while growing up , besides always having to clean their own rooms they had to help clean the house, they had to do Laundry which I had to do too so there was not difference there , but the worst part was what my oldest sister , actually the three oldest once had to endure , they had been old enough to see all the bad things that happened during their flight from the Russians they had seen things that some of us never get to see in all our life, it had made them a bit bitter ,because when I came along there was piece , my Mother had much more time to spend with me than ever having had for any one of them , so naturally , the bad feelings between them and myself started growing . Knowing now what my Mother meant by not stooping down to their level but also why my sisters behaved the way they did , seeing that me being the last of the children got more attention from my mom , also she was not so strict any more ,besides that , from now on I would not fight with any one of them any more , so many times they tempted me but walking away from their insinuations was the smart way to handle this . Also my oldest sister did not hit me any more so one good thing came out of that conflict , she left me alone , but now she would be verbally abusing me but since my Mother had died the only thing that could get to me if she would say something bad about my mom . Ever so often thinking about my Mother as we had arrived in Calgary , was wondering how she would handle this situation right now ,being here without knowing any one no Family or Friends it was not easy for me since not speaking English at the beginning . It all went better in time but wanting to go home , back to Germany was very much on my mind , a few times I had already booked a flight home but one of the children got sick and they did not permit me to take that child on to the plain , that went on for the first six months , thinking back now it must have been Gods will , not letting me go back home . Calgary was a big City but a very clod one , most of the People here where not to friendly towards new combers but that did not bother me half as much as the fact that the Schools where not so good ,

Claudia needed to be in grad three , but was put in one , Dieter & Joerg where also in the same grade , needless to say my Daughter did not like to be in the same class with her brothers, since she had been already through all the reading and writing which they just started to do now . Often the wish to go back crept up in my mind and telling my husband that we would leave as soon as everything was right for us to go back , but he told me that he was not willing to go back with us , he had changed , just as I had feared he would . There was nothing about that sweet Man who used to tell me that he would do anything for me , what happened to him , asking my husband one day as he behaved stupid again , what is going on with you ,did you just wanted me to come along with the kids so you would not be alone ? He looked at me , how can you say that , " well very easy , since we have been here you have changed a lot, not only do you not go with us anywhere, any more ,but also you treat me like a stranger sometimes . It is only because that I worry about a Job he, said , having to look after the children and you it is not going to be easy , ' that my friend you knew when we still where in Germany right "? But now all of a sudden this is not so good any more , let me tell you this , the children and I will go back to Germany you can stay here the divorce Papers will be send to you since we got Married in Belgium that should not be a problem !" Looking at me like someone had done something wrong to him , why would you leave , he said , the reason we got married was that because I love you and still do very much so , also the kids are my life now , without all of you there is no reason for me to stay here is there ? You tell me I said , but if that is the case than you better change your behavior towards me and the children because that Plain with us on board will leave here any time we like to leave . We had been here all but two weeks when we had this talk ,but tomorrow I would start to work , finding a job for me was easy if wanting to do Office cleaning , since never having done that , it was as believed to be easy for me , but it was not at first ,but it was okay after a few weeks ,it seemed like this was what needed to be done . The best thing about that, was being, home in the day time for the children then at five in the afternoon walking downtown was not so good , not speaking English to much yet I could not tell the bus driver where to let me of the bus, so walking to work and back home was my only option at this time . One ,day after about two months we had the middle of June walking home having the strange feeling that something was not right . Hope fully all was well at home , walking faster made it not go away either but my Husband was coming towards me already while walking up that last hill , is everything okay ? Not really he said , Claudia is not feeling to well she has very bad stomach pains ,what kind of Doctor can we find at this time of night , well there must be an emergency number one could call , they probably know where to go . By that time we had arrived at home and Claudia was feeling better , a friend that we had made who lived right across from us , she was a Native Indian Lady by the name of Doreen , she had sat with the children while Peter was coming to get me , she had given Claudia some Tea that she had made herself and my daughter was feeling much better . For the next little while, we had told Claudia if those pains come back to tell us right away , but it seemed to be okay for now . The whole reason of me working was that we wanted to have some kind of income until Peter would have found a Job as an Engineer , he was getting very restless , afraid there might not be anything here in Calgary for him . If my gut feeling had told me what would be in store for me here , in a strange Land I would not be here at all , but God knows what he does , honestly he does, because he thought me that it was okay to feel scared , okay to feel alone and helpless because what that meant was , in the future those feelings would all disappear and one was much stronger for it . One thing was for sure to me after the first two ,years , it was okay to fight for what one believed to be right , and it was okay to be nice to people , also to show them that one had feelings just like the next person . In Germany a lot of the People who knew me always believed that I was stuck up as they say , but in fact it was my shield my safety coat not to have to show them that I was afraid of meeting new people and very much afraid of making mistakes having to admit that I was not perfect . Here in Canada , all of that was not necessary , because nobody gave a hoot if I was scared or any of those other things , the main thing here was , to be honest , to show that one was just human and felt just as the next guy or girl . It was also okay to make mistakes if one did not , how could one learn about to make them right ? God had his plan alright , he sure did , specially with me because having the hardest time in my life ,back home always saying that my sisters should not come to my house because it was fine without them but here , how much I wished for one of them to walk through my front door, only God knew . So many times , the wish was so strong that sitting down remembering how mean one had been to me or the other way around did not seem important at all any more , we where sisters and that is what mattered ! So needless to say a lot of letters where written in the first two years and never did my sisters mean more to me as in that time , the letters coming back where just full of apologizing words and we love you any way and so on that we on both ends needed to cry a lot to forgive all the things we had said and done to one another . Having sisters again made my life in Canada a bit easier even if it was not perfect between us but it was much better than it ever had been , my mother would have been very proud of me , every time thinking of her made me very sad so much so that crying a lot made my children worry , the first one to say something was Dieter , why are you crying all the time mom, he asked me one day , not having been aware of the fact that the children had seen me cry , now being ashamed that letting them see me like that . It was just not fair to them and the last thing that one wanted was having the children worry , they had become so happy we taken them every Weekend out of town , on little trips, it was very nice , as much as we did not like Calgary we loved the surroundings all the more , the Mountains where visible in the back ground and every time we had enough money for Gasoline we would drive to Banff or to the Rocky Mountains , they where so magnificent , every time we hiked there it felt like getting closer to God up on the Mountain meadow . The children loved to go on trips because every time we went we saw some wild animals which we never seen before , except in a Zoo ,like the white Mountain Goats with there little once or the Mountain sheep, the Moose, Elk as well as Black Bears and Grizzly . To my boys it was like an adventure all the time, even in the winter we would drive to Banff because there was a lot of snow for tobogganing which we all liked to do very much . It was now the beginning of August, all had been going well , Peter had found a job as an Engineer in a Company who where building off Road Vehicles . great big once, they also build the Columbia Ice Field Bus .

Everything going so well only this day when I got home my daughter Claudia was not doing well ,she was in pain again only this time there was no waiting around we needed to go to the Hospital . We had found a children's specialist downtown in the Calgary Tower but when phoning him he told me to go straight to the Hospital he would meet us there . My guess was that my baby had her appendix giving her problems , it was painful and being only eight years old in a strange country she was not to keen on going to the Hospital ,but assuring her that I would stay with her no matter what, she was okay . Arriving there was fast , all we had to do, go down 16th Avenue which also was the Highway one, going right from Banff all the way through Calgary to the East . In the Foothills Hospital our Child specialist was waiting already , he escorted us to the place where we needed to go with her , by now she had passed out once again, because of the pain and it was high time for an operation , it brought back a lot of memories , it was like I was lying there only thing different was I had been nine years old, one year older than my sweetie . Having the, Doctor there was somewhat reassuring , but he would not operate on her we where told , there was another specialist he would do the operation, but he needed to talk to us before doing so . First he had examine her , after that he came out to let us know when he would operate , but he had a different surprise for us too , telling us that one of Claudia's intestines had a knot in it which had to be operated as well, he would do both in the same operation that way she did not have to come back . We where quite surprised but if the knot was there all the time , I had to ask the Doctor , could that have had anything to do with her not eating enough ? Yes, it most certainly would ,he said because the food can not go out of the other side of the stomach with this knot being right there . Now we felt really bad because we had scolded her lot of times because she did not want to eat , naturally thinking she did not want the food we put in front of her , finding out now that she could not help that was hard for me , since loving my children so much naturally, it was only to be for their own good if asked to eat once food before them . But when she was operated I would apologize to her that was for sure , needless to say I was all alone with Claudia at the Hospital , Peter had to work late and could not come with me , the boys where at home too, my friend Doreen was looking after them until Peter would get home . Going home that night was out of the question , Claudia would be devastated if she woke up and her mom was not there, besides , leaving her there all alone was just not on my mind , it was not done where I came from, one would stay with their child no doubt about that . While she was being Operated I had time to pray once again asking ," God , please let Claudia be okay , let her get well soon and have not too much pain after , and God if you are there please look after the Boys and Peter tonight they are alone, help them to sleep make sure that they are okay , and thank you very much for letting us get here in time , in Jesus name I pray , Amen . Now feeling like the whole world was upon my shoulders because every time there was anything wrong Peter was not there , he rather worked, even if he did not have to, understanding to a point that he wanted his Boss to see what he could do for the Company , besides that, it was to our advantage , even so , he should have been there with me he never was any more ,ever since we had left Germany he seemed to be another person . Thinking this did not make me to happy ,but when the Nurse came to let me know that

Claudia was okay she was just brought in to her Room , the operation went well she said and your child is doing great . Thank you God , was my silent prayer , walking behind the nurse to the room my daughter was in I was talking to God again , since we where here I did that a lot, there was nobody else there for me to talk to unless I counted my Dad when I phoned him in Germany . That reminded me to let him know about Claudia, he did not know yet ,everything had happened so fast .Staying over night with my daughter was good, she had a restless night , it was good to hold her little hands in mine she would calm down as soon as she felt my hand , the whole night she had been having bad dreams I guess ,but in the morning she was okay , having a great ,breakfast with her I needed to go home and bring some clothes for her, also some of her books and her favorite doll . Would you be okay if I went home for a little while , that way I could get some of your things and bring them to you ,the boys need to have lunch today too so I make them some lunch okay ? But as soon as everything is done I am back here with you okay ? That is okay Mom she said hurry back , her eyes had some tears in them but she pretended not to be afraid to be alone , yet I knew that she was terrified to stay there alone . Naturally ,as fast as was possible running home was only three miles , the first two uphill but it was okay the only thing was, I needed to go to work in the afternoon, would there be time enough to spend with my daughter before going , may be Peter could go with the boys to stay with her for a while until I got back after work . Asking the nurses if it was okay to stay one more night, because Claudia could come home the third day after the operation , but that would mean someone had to stay home with her, it would be me of course , there was no use to ask

Peter he would say no any way. On my way home all kinds of things went through my mind why did Peter change so much, what has happened between then and now, to ask him was useless since trying that before ,but getting not a satisfactory answer at all, there needed to be a good talking between the two of us or truly ,I would leave him here and go home to Germany, it might be for the best of all of us. At home there was nobody there yet but Doreen had seen me walking up to my house she came right over, the boys had a good breakfast and if you like they can come to my house for lunch, would you do that, it would be such a great help ,just came home to get some things for Claudia than make some supper for Peter and the boys and then go back to the Hospital .You should ask Peter to help out ,you know, she said, knowing that she was right but not saying anything more about it, changing the subject to , I might have to stay home a few days when Claudia is home, she can not go to School for the next two weeks the doctor said , just hope that they give me a few days off. But of course there was no time to talk about that to much, there was only time to cook and clean the house and take some of Claudia's things back to the Hospital . The fact that Doreen would look after the boys was a good feeling ,at least there was one friend one could count on . Arriving at the Hospital again the Doctor was in with Claudia , as he saw me coming he told me that she needed to be home for three weeks not two ,also that she was not to climb , run ,jump or do any other things like that ,but keep her very still and be careful not to do to much at first . Knowing all of that from my own experience , asking Claudia if she wanted something from the cafeteria she said yes , " what would you like .just some fruit mom but no grapes, the Doctor said ,those are not

good right now for me, in case they have pits in them , that was known to me too ,I had the same thing told to me when my appendix was taken out . Isn't life funny , exactly the same things had been told to me years ago , like Mother like Daughter , well what else would life hold for me today ? To get to work from the Hospital , there was no way for me to know which bus needed to be taken, so walking was on the agenda once more , but feeling not so good I did not walk as fast as usual , what was wrong with me ,why this strange feeling and the pain , my appendix was none existent any more, but what about those pains , every few minutes . Going in to the Building where cleaning the offices for the last few months ,was what my job was , there was the other lady who cleaned the floor above mine , asking her about the time of might be a good idea ,may be she could help me to ask the right person . Who do I ask about getting a few days off , she just looked at me , how long have you been here ,well about three months now, but my daughter is in the Hospital she had an operation, she is going to come home tomorrow or the next day , I need to be home for her . Well if you would only need a few days that would be okay but not three weeks , that is not done ,after all, you only work part time at night . How can that be done then, my daughter needs me at home and she come first and foremost , so do my other two children , as much as I need this job, but not so badly for leaving my children to fend for themselves . The only thing you can do than is to quit and come back when she is better and gone back to School , quit , that is what you are telling me , by now speaking English was not a problem for me any more ,of course there was a lot that I needed to learn , but this conversation was okay for me, to understand that this was not a job I would be doing any more . My, children had always come first and this would be no different. Having said that after having finished cleaning made my way up to the Hospital again ,but not before phoning home to make sure that Peter was home tonight , he was , telling him what had been said to me about the days off, he was not happy about the fact that now he was the only provider for a few weeks, making a big deal out of nothing again, so I just hang up the phone . By now I began to think that Peter only wanted me to come with him because he did not want to be alone in a strange ,Country ,my gut feeling told me so, and probably right fully so but if that was the case than I knew what needed to be done . Coming in to Claudia's room Peter was there already , because hanging up on him was not done before ,so he was afraid that I might do something that he did not want me to do . Why did you hang up on me, he asked , "that surprises you ,how come you never have time for us ,or for me , you never ever help me with anything any more, what do you think this is, a one man band , why did you want me to go with you at all ? By now we had left the room and where standing in the hallway , the boys where in with their sister ,they had a lot to talk about School , so did Peter and myself . He was just looking at me, not understanding or not wanting to , well this is it , arrangements will be made for the Children and I to go home to Germany, we have some Money put aside, tomorrow the tickets will be bought and you can live here and do what you want . Until now you have not helped me once with anything you are the one who can speak English ,but I was the one who had to go to all the Offices, for our Insurance cards and Identifications , that we needed for here, you never even helped me with my learning for the drivers license here , Doreen had to help me . How do you think that makes me feel, going everywhere all alone , you did not even come to the Hospital the first night when Claudia was operated on , why did you need to stay at the Office longer that night, you had told me there was no overtime for anyone at all ? By now ,his face had turned white but that did not mean anything Peter could not stand Hospitals, neither was he any good in talking things over, he only did his thing and that was it, but now this was the time to say something ,if he wanted me to stay with him, if he did not ,then that would be the end of this . The reason of staying at the office longer than usual was that we are working on a new Columbia Ice Field Bus , one without chains , we are almost done, but that was the reason , " and you could not tell me that the other day when asking you about it ? By now the feeling that I have is such that you do not care about any one of us, most of all not for me , because your behavior has been as if you do not give a hoot about anything any more since we got here .You care just about your self ! Being very aggressive towards Peter was not like me , what was wrong , of course being mad at him was one thing ,but like this , it was not like me to be this bad , but for once that was okay , he needed to be told, because we have been here now for four months and not once did he go with me anywhere, so what should I make of that ? While we where standing there this pain came back again and bending over seemed to help it go away a little bit, but one of the nurses who had come by asked me if everything was okay ? No it is not , hearing myself say ,that was what made her come closer , where is the pain , well right here , pointing at my stomach the pain was so bad that nearly fainting was one thing, the other was , sitting on the floor but that did not help a lot . Oh God , talking to him always helped me a lot so now too , please I can not get sick , Claudia is coming home tomorrow she needs me, please let me be okay ! The Nurse did not wait any longer, she called one of the Orderlies to come and bring a Wheelchair for me , than they brought me downstairs in to the examination rooms . One of the boys came out of Claudia's room , it was Dieter he got very scared as he saw they had me in that chair and where about to bring me away, he started crying , please let me take my son with me down okay ,he is very upset that you are taking me away from up here . Okay ,she said ,you can come but you have to wait outside the Curtain you understand that ? Yes, he did , the surprising thing was that my children knew more about the English language than I did , they learned by playing with the neighbor children . Doreen had helped me a lot by having me sit down two hours every day and speak English to her, she would correct me if necessary but most at the time she would make up a sentence and have me repeat it , that helped me a lot . Going down on this Elevator the pain was very bad, I had not eaten anything today except with Claudia this morning, so may be it was my stomach telling me that there needed to be some food coming down soon, who knows ,but it was not that as we found out later . Dieter was crying the whole time he was afraid that his mom had to stay in the Hospital , but telling him that I would not stay here no matter what , seemed to be the trick, he stopped crying but held on to my hand the whole time until I had to go behind the curtain . Not showing my son   how much worry this was causing me , keeping up a brave face ,was very important , knowing that he always was such a Mamas boy , he was worried about me all the time since his Father had beat me up and he got hurt too ,he knew what it meant to hurt . Any way ,after the Doctor had finished his examination   he asked me , how many children do you have , three was the answer , well than get ready for number four , you are going to have another child , the pain is what that means, you are pregnant , but why this pain , well he said sometimes when the egg does not go through right away or another one wants to go where the first one has gotten already too , than it can cause these pains but only for a little while ,may be till tomorrow, but as far as we can tell you , you must be pregnant all the tests show this . Please , do not tell my Husband just yet he is upstairs with my Daughter she had been operated on her appendix , may be after we get home I can tell him . To find out   that   one is pregnant is not a good thing right now , why God , asking him was the only thing for me to do right now ,what else was there to do . For me it was actually a nice feeling, since loving children always was my thing , one more would not make a big difference to me . Claudia would be very happy she always told me that she would like to have a little sister . But now what , just having told Peter that I was going back to Germany with the children , there was no way that telling him was an option ,he would not find out until we where back in Germany , me and the kids . Now it all made sense to me too, being in such a bad mood was usually not my thing ,but for the past few weeks it had been very bad ,even if saying so myself . Going up to see Claudia and telling her was not going to be done today either, I would wait until Peter was not there and then tell all three of them, also let them know we would be going home soon to see their Grandfather and all their relatives again . Having thought this when walking in to Claudia's room Peter was not there any more , he had told her to let me know that he would be home with Joerg and waiting for me to come home , we needed to talk about something . Looking at my daughter, asking her how she was feeling ,she told me that the Doctor had told her she would be able to go home tomorrow , are you going to be home with me Mommy she asked , yes sweetie, I am looking forward to having to spend a lot of time with you, in the past few months your mom was always very busy, doing everything ,going to work and all but now it will be just the three of you and me if that is okay with you . She had the biggest smile on her face so did my son Dieter , can we go to one of those McDonalds places we have heard so much about , we would like to go there just one time Mom . Please , as every one knows having two pairs of eyes looking at you very sad , there is no way one can say no to them, this Mother sure could not , what the hey , we are going to go to one okay, I promise, but now you have to promise me something too , you know what I found out downstairs what is wrong with me , both started to look scared again , oh no it is nothing bad do not worry okay , it is truly nothing bad, but we will have another addition to the Family may be a girl or a boy . Claudia's eyes lit up like a fireball , she could make her eyes just sparkle when she was excited , oh mom she wanted to get out of her bed to give me a big hug , but I was faster ,bending over to here giving her a warm kiss on her cheeks and then a big hug , as well as turning to Dieter who had come closer to give his mom a big hug , both of them looked so happy , but we can not let Peter know, not at all because we are going back to Germany the four of us Peter is going to stay here . How will that be Mom they both looked at me kind of sad , we thought that we would stay a family , yes so did I but it does not work , if I have to do all the work that can not be, Peter always worked late even telling me that they would not have anybody working over time, I do not know what to make of his behavior, so please not a word to him or Joerg just yet okay ? Two faces looking at me like little Sherlock Holmes , we can keep a secret honestly we can , Claudia turning towards Dieter , you better not tell Joerg or he will tell Peter , pinky swear that you do not tell either one of them she said , Dieter had no choice he had to swear too . We stayed for two more hours as it was dark already Dieter and I walked home, it was a long walk for a six year old but he did not complain , if you can do this so can I he said to me , looking up at me, his little face smiling at me , can we go tomorrow to get one of those Hamburgers we heard so much about ? May be, we have to wait and see how Claudia is feeling, we need to take a Taxi tomorrow to pick her up , than we see okay ? That was fine by him ,he held on to my hand very strongly as if to say , I am here for you Mom . He was such a good little Man , he was always worried about me , unlike my Husband ,he never thought twice about either the kids or me, just his job was what he had in mind , well he could have that and only that, one can not have it both ways and a Marriage is a Partnership , where two people help each other to cope with all the things that come their way ,but up to now , the only one who was coping was myself ,Peter always needed to be somewhere else when he was needed . Enough of that ,those kind of things don't need to be going on in my mind right now , there was a much nicer thing to be thinking about and that was the new baby . What would it look like , up to now Joerg was the only one who looked like my side of the family ,may be this new one would do too , may be like my Mom or one of my brothers , that would be great , thinking of back home made me smile , how would they all react when we got back . Still smiling when walking in the door ,at our house Joerg was sitting at the dinner table waiting for us to come home, the table was set, there was a smell of Hamburger in the house , Peter had gone out to get us Hamburgers and French fries also everybody got a Milkshake . We have waited for you Mom , Joerg said , look Dad got us all some Hamburgers , these where the first once since we got to Canada ,never wanted to buy them because to me they where not real food ,or very good nutrition , but I guess today was the day we would have some . Why did you buy those , turning to Peter , asking him , because Joerg asked me on the way home if we could have some at least once and they do not look so bad , the fries look good too, but you should taste those Milk shakes they are out of this world . Having said that he pulled out a chair for me , Dieter sat down already , only Claudia was missing , thinking of her being all alone in the Hospital was not such a good feeling ,but she would be home by tomorrow night . That meal was not bad at all , my Husband had done something nice for the children that was good , but it did not make me forget what we had talked about, good thing he did not know about the baby , just don't know what he would say ,but hoping he would not find out until we would be at the Airport and on the way home . But that was not to be , once more God did not want me to go , as a matter of fact he wanted me to humble myself , and to understand that only he tells me what to do, and what not ,as we all where enjoying our shakes the conversation took another turn , Peter just out right asked the two boys if they are happy here at all , yes we are ,the best part is when we all drive to Banff Dieter said ,and when we go hiking up the Mountain , that is so much fun and next year we can take the baby with us , oh sorry Mom , he looked at me very sad that he had betrayed my confident in him , he had sworn not to say anything but by rights he did noting wrong . Telling him that it was okay to tell ,because it was not nice of me not to tell Peter , he smiled , would it not be nice to have a little brother ? Hopefully it would be a sister, because that is what Claudia would like to have, Joerg said ,Peter did not say anything ,he just sat there looking at me as if looking at a stranger , why did you not want to tell me about this when was I supposed to hear about it ? Well as we had been talking at the Hospital the trip home for me and the children will be booked next week, we are going home ,you have shown me nothing of a good family life , all you have done is behaved as if you are single ,and now you can do that for the rest of your life , we will not be in your way, neither will you get to see or hear about this baby , also you do not have to worry about having to pay for it , believe me you do not, up to now I have always been very capable to look after my children . That is just it he said , you had to do this for some years now, you can not let me do anything at all , every time that I offer my help you tell me it is not necessary , but afterwards you complain because you had to do it alone ,why won't you admit that you would like me to help you at least once in a while ? Is it really so hard for you to rely on someone else for a change , just admit that you need help sometimes too , that is all I want and it is okay to ask for help believe me . He got up from his chair and came around the table where I was sitting , now tell me about this baby , there is no way that you will go back to Germany without me , we either stay all here, or we all go back , that is that .He put his arms around me telling me how much he loved me and the children , there is no way I could be without either one of you, don't you see that ? His eyes told the story and knowing that they could not lie , promised him to think about it , that was the least that I could do right now .

Having had this out in the open now, the realization set in that there would be another baby , what about my new job , while in the Hospital one of the Nurses had asked me if that kind of work in there would interest me , of course it would ,but how would I get a job there ? Well she said , all you have to do go down the Administration Office and fill out an application , you have to name someone who is know by the Hospital or any of our Staff may be you could ask around ,but we are only here for four months now we don't know anybody as of yet . That is not a problem just write this name down , she gave me a piece of paper on which there was a name , that we did not know, but if she believed it would help than this one would be on my application that was for sure . Now sitting here at home , Peter and the boys where cleaning up the table , there was a feeling of hope that all would get better , my Mothers voice again , just keep your self healthy , than the baby will be big and strong , meanwhile be happy ,Peter is a good man he is going to look after all of you well, there is no need for you to worry about the future , with God by your side , all of you will be fine . If only it was that easy ,but I was thinking about a lot of times when all hope was lost , now this , a new baby what a present ,which luck for me , Peter still had not said anything about the baby ,may be he did not want another one, probably would tell me when the boys are in bed but if it is bad news he can just keep it to himself . Some things are best left alone while others need to be out in the open , Claudia got out of Hospital the next morning Peter brought the boys and me down he told me not to walk but take a Taxi , we would have done that any way .Claudia could not walk this distance , there was no way , but she was so happy to see us and she did not know that we had told Peter about the baby , but leave it to Dieter , he loved his sister very much one could tell so he went first thing when we got in to her room to tell her about last night . How did Dad take that Mom she asked , well actually very well , but he has not told me yet if he is happy about that or not . Don't worry he will, just give him some time , this was an eight year old , well soon to be nine next month ,but still she was so happy about me being pregnant as if she was the Mother . Time went by fast ,Claudia recovered quickly and we all where waiting for the baby to arrive Christmas had come and gone now it was the beginning of May again , the children where doing great in school , Claudia was in her regular grade that she should be in , Dieter & Joerg where in grade two which was a boost for the both of them but there was no more problem with English for any one of them ,just for me it was a bit hard sometimes , but that would be okay I had a good Teacher , Doreen , she was like a ray of sunshine to me , specially when one does not know to many people , in my case nobody , one is very glad to have someone like her by her side . She always made me sit down with her , went over and over on some of the subjects that I was having problems with, never tired of my questions . So this one day , being at her house we had just started to learn when I fell of the chair . This was the 20 day of May 75 , the baby was not due for another two weeks and there was no pain , just fallen of the chair . Naturally Doreen got very scared she phoned my Doctor and he wanted us to come right down to his office , on the way there I was feeling very dizzy but could not explain that at all , why would that be with the other three children there was never anything like this or any other thing ,now what was going on ?

After the examination, the doctor explained to us , that it is not unusual for a woman to faint when she is pregnant ,some women have that phenomenon early in the pregnancy but others sometimes on the last day or so , but since there was no pain involved there was nothing to worry about , just make sure you take it easy a bit okay ? That was not so good , how could one take it easy, having to look after three children and a Husband who was very demanding when it came to his food or clothes ,but he had been a Soldier and used to everything nice and clean . Any way ,all would be well that was for sure, the baby was in the right position as he told us , the heartbeat was normal and all should go swimmingly . He smiled when we where on the way out and asked me to stay for a minute , you know of course Monika that you can not have your baby at home , here in Calgary ,there are no Midwifes here , neither would the healthcare let you stay home it is not done here , are you okay with that . Dr.Motta ,I have to be okay with that do I not , but it will be hard on me to go to the Hospital , one thing is for sure , that I wait till the last minute you can count on that . Well , stay alert rest a little bit more okay ,we do not want any complications . Never had any with the other three ,what makes you think this one would be different ? One never knows, he said ,because every baby is different from the one before and don't forget it has been six years since you had the last one, it will be just like having the first one . Thank you for your concern it is appreciated , and we will rest a bit more okay ? That is my girl he said , he always said that to all the woman who came in here , but he was a great Doctor and we all liked him very much .Few weeks later we had a little boy , his name was Peter but not just because of my Husband , but also thinking about the two peters who where followers of Jesus, they had been good guys and I wanted this for my son to be as well . God must have known that because Peter junior was the highlight of our life ,not just for us but also for Claudia , Dieter & Joerg , they all had and have a very good relationship , even if I do not ,but making sure that always telling them time after time to stick together, which they now do . It was a great time, going back to work after Peter junior was about four months old that was the time when we needed the money the most , the older children where growing up faster than one had thought , but not only that, we needed to find a different house ,this first one was too small , it was okay for the start but now there was a new one needed badly . Calgary was a Cow town at the time when we got there, it still is and most of the People there do not like children or animals except Horses and Cows , so when phoning around to find out about one or the other house that we had found out about in the paper, we always got a no, as soon as we mentioned the children . Four children was too much they all said, but just as we where giving up there was God again , one night the children where in bed , we where both looking through some of the Papers we had just picked up that day , as we where talking about nobody wanting any children in their House we came across an add that said Children welcome . Loosing no time I went to the phone knowing full well that it was nine o'clock at night ,but that was not important to me right now , just this add , children wanted , that was some kind of important thing to me .Answering the phone was a Woman , she introduced herself as Joyce Vollmerhaus , sorry to call you so late in the day, but we just found your add in today's Paper , is the House still available ? Yes it is, if you like , you can come over tomorrow and take a look . How many children have you got , four three are in School the last one is just a baby . There was a pause on the other end , now it comes we thought, the answer is, no sorry, not that many , but instead we heard her say, that is fine, we see you tomorrow about six then ? Yes we will , be there you can count on that, thank you very much for your time , sorry again for disturbing you at such a late hour . Not at all she said ,we always are up quite late there is no problem . We could not believe that , Peter looked at me ,what if they tell us no when we get there tomorrow ,when they see the children , not to worry Dieter and Joerg have told me that they will be on their best behavior and Claudia is any way , junior is the best one of all of them, you know that, so there is nothing to worry about . Peter junior was a very quiet child , just like his father , my husband was also very quiet that was what I loved so much about him , only would say something if he had an important message for all of us ,other than that he did not talk very much . Next day we could not wait for Peter to get home , the children and I where ready to go , dinner had to wait ,this was much more important to miss out on , what if they truly did love children, that house we saw was a five bedroom house , everybody would have their own room , just perfect . As Peter was driving up to our   House , Dieter was running out already ,telling him that we could go right now , okay that is good he said lets get in the car then and go . We just looked at the House from the Road at first , it looked very nice and clean , driving around in to the back alley, we had a parking spot right in the back yard , getting out of the Car , the children where very happy to see that there was a big Garden , where they had a Cement round close to the house .Being very big Joerg suggested it to be for a Swimming Pool for them ,but Peter said it was for a Clothes line one of those spider looking things to hang up clothes on . Since we where their first we had time to go around the house to the front which was very nice , high up away from the road we never forget, it was white with red blinds around the windows the kind they have in Germany , may be these people are German Peter said to me ,. May be they are ,but this Joyce Person sounded like a Canadian , as we came around to the back yard , somebody was there already, asking us how we liked the house , it looks great I could hear myself saying , just enough room for the children , this would be perfect for us , looking at the Lady who told us her name was Joyce, we hope you also like the inside, because we would like you to have this house . That was a statement we where not prepared for at all , it usually went like this , " thank you for coming by but we do not take families with so many children sorry ."This time it was so different , of course you must see the inside first Joyce said , and my Husband will be along shortly to bring the papers for you to sign so you can move in whenever you want . Having heard that but not believing it , I could hear my self ask Joyce , are you sure you would like to give us this house to rent , after all we have these four children ,so what she said , that is no reason for me not to let you have this house , there is a lot of room for all of them , is there not ? Oh yes that is thru but up to now we had nothing but no for answers , from the people ,as soon as they heard on the phone that we had four children . Well she said , those are the kind of people you do not want to rent from any way ,they all have forgotten that they had been children at one point in time, but we do love children and have nothing against them, or you for that matter . Lets go inside to take a look ,may be you do not like this inside , but she was wrong , the inside was just as clean as the outside the rooms where nice and bright , lots of windows ,big rooms upstairs as well as down the boys each had their room picked out by the time Joyce's husband came and to our surprise he was German, he heard us talking in our own language and fell right in just to let us know that he understood what we where saying . His name was Walter and he was a Mathematic Professor at the University in Calgary . How much luck can we get Peter said , it has very little to do with luck ,but our prayers have been answered , the children have prayed with me for so long already , for us to find a nice house , where we could be happy and Claudia did not have to be afraid any more, now we found it ,actually it found us . The new Landlords are very nice , that is not , luck but Gods work believe me , if not for him ,this would not be available for us right now . Walter was asking us, if we would like to sign the Papers , there is not question we love to sign them , when can we move in ? Tonight ,tomorrow ,whenever you are ready , the House is empty, there is nothing to be done , so it is ready to be lived in for you, here is the key , but we would like for you to come up to our House, it is right up the next road , just so you know where we are in case anything needs to be done on this house ,you can drop by and tell us, if that is okay with you ! Okay with us , what a question, we love to go with you, after having gotten the okay for this house, the key in my hand felt nice and warm , how long are you planning on living in this house Walter asked Peter , only until we have build our own , we are saving up to build a House but it wont be before two or three years yet , because of Peter junior he threw us back a little bit financially , but that does not matter , we still are building our own soon . Glad to hear that, Walter said , but for however long you need this house, it is for you to use any way you like it . How come you are so kind to People with children , not usually he said but with you , just by looking at your children, the way they behaved , they listened to you right away and they all took their shoes of going in to the house, that showed me what kind of People you are, that is why you are getting this house .Walking up to their house we could hear a dog bark , it sounded like a big dog, going around the house with us in to their back yard, we saw this beautiful German Sheppard , what a great dog I said, bending down to pet him ,you are not afraid of him ,Walter asked ,never have been afraid of any dog in my life . We always had a lot of animals around us when growing up , the last dog we had was a Sheppard too ,just like this one only, ours had different colors . Alex ,was the name of the dog, he took to me right away, much to the surprise of his owners ,but then most dog liked me , wherever we went dogs would always come up to me , but also to Peter, we both loved animals . We where invited to have a bit of a supper with Joyce and Walter , where we told them how long we had been here, why we are here and what we are doing for work , listening to me Joyce said ,you are working outside the house , yes ever since we got here ,only stayed home for a month after junior was born but now I work at the Medical School aside the Foothills Hospital , you should try to get in to the University they pay much more and you get three weeks of summer holidays right the first year . Really , that would be something to look in to , how can I ask or whom to ask would be a better question .Any time there was more money mentioned it was good to find out more about that because we are saving up to buy a House or build one , there is a lot of Money needed and with Peter's Paycheck alone it would not be enough . For a while we where telling them how or why we came to Canada also that we had good jobs in Germany , but there was a good reason why we did have to come here or Australia , for that matter , not telling the whole story just enough so they would understand the reason for us to come here . On the way home in the car Peter was very happy , almost too much so , there was something else he needed to tell me but he was waiting for us to be in the car , he did not want Joyce or Walter to hear this . Now what is it asking him, while the children where talking about this new home we would live in , they where so glad to get out of that small house but actually , I liked that small house it was our first home here in Canada and it had a very big back yard ,the kids where always running ,playing in it , there was a lot of room . Any way , by Peters face it must be something very good or he would not look like this ,and it was , well he started , today I was called in to the Office from my boss, he wanted to let me know that there would be a bonus for me in my next paycheck , because I had come up with a new idea about a Columbia Ice Field Bus , instead of having Chains , now we can have one with Tires only, but the right tires , we had build it already, they used it two days ago on the Ice Fields for the first time and it works great . Not only do we get a bonus but also more Pay from now on , two hundred and forty dollars every month , wow , that was all that came out of my mouth , how come you did not tell me about this new bus sooner , it would have been nice to know before ,. We where not permitted to tell anybody since this company is the first one to build one like this ,they got a big contract because of that from the Government, just because , and that is why we, who had worked on this project ,are all getting more money from now on !

    News like that was so good to hear , up to now we had to struggle very hard , it is not easy with four children, plus we came here with three small kids ,now a fourth one is there ,we both where working , when Peter gets home I have to leave home , since working at the Medical School I work from five to two in the morning , get up at six with Peter again to make breakfast for everybody . Any way it was great news and for the fun of it we went to , 'Peters Drive In ', a small Hamburger place ,but they had the best fries there and truly the best Hamburgers . It was not often that we would eat like that ,very seldom but today was a special day , not only did we get a great House but also we would have more money in our purse, that sounded very good . That night my prayers where very long thanking God for all that had happened today , for his generosity towards us , to have us meet Joyce and Walter two very nice People, actually the first nice once we had met until now . Also thanking him for all he had done for us up to now , asking him to guide us on our journey, and what ever he wanted us to do , we should do , but at the same time , bring us good luck for the children, more so , keep them save God , do not let anybody lay a hand on any one of them , look after them where ever they may go . On our trip's please be beside us , go with us so we are returning home save . It went on for quit some time I had the feeling that with every prayer there was another one that needed to be said , another thing needed to be asked of God , him who had brought us so much happiness today . By the time I was finished , falling asleep was not in, so hearing Peter snore beside me I got up to sit out back on the porch , then I heard some foot steps behind me , it was my daughter Claudia , you can't sleep either mom , no sweetie but you should be asleep you have School tomorrow . Just wanted to talk to you about our new School , we hope it is a nice one and the Teachers there are good and nice to us , why would you say this , looking at her she said , because some of the once in this school are not nice to us , they call us names sometimes , who and which once please tell me , after she had told me she went inside to her room , but I was still sitting out there thinking of how stupid can a Teacher be to be calling children names , how old is this Teacher , well I would see tomorrow because this is not going to be unpunished where this Mother is concerned . Next morning after everybody had left , I phoned the School Principal telling him that there is a matter that needed to be discussed between us, that it needed to be done this morning or I would go to the School Board . Well if it is urgent than please come by right now he said , okay that suits me fine in a few minutes we can talk , hanging up the phone making sure all the doors where looked taking junior in his carriage , off we went ! The School was only one block away from the house we lived in , it took only a few minutes for me to reach the School , but by now this mom was very mad, and when she was , watch out people, because if it was about my children I was like a Grizzly Bear , ready to lash out at anybody who was at fault . Now the Principal did not believe me at first, but he called my three children to his Office, asking them why they had not come to him with this, he looked at Claudia , why did you not come to me , this kind of behavior from a Teacher is not permitted , it should not have happened ,but since it did, I said , there will be punishment .Because I did already phone the School Board , this is not going to be swept under the table for all I am concerned . He did not like what I was saying , but had to agree , that it was not a good behavior towards the children . The Teacher who was in question was called in to the Office as well , when she saw the children her face turned a different color, but when she saw me it went all white . Well have you got any excuse for your self , by calling those children the names you did call them , he did not ask her if she had done so but told her that she had , with that showing the children he believed them and not her . At first she did not know what to say, but then admitted to the fact , but also said that it was only in fun , now that was my cue . In fun, how would you like it if I hit you in the mouth right now and then told you it was only for fun ? How can you ,being a grown up, be so insensitive towards a child that is dependent on you for guidance here in School , how can you expect them to have any respect for you at all . My children have been thought to respect all grown ups because they deserve to have that respect ,but with you in mind, now they wont because you have shown them how stupid a Teacher can be . For the rest of the Teachers they wont have respect either because they stand by you which showed my children that they agree with your behavior towards them . This is going to the School board believe me, than we will see what they do about that , after that it will be in the Calgary Herald for the next two weeks, because going there this afternoon and having them put it in there to make sure you never do this to any other children ever again . Turning to the Principal , today is the last day my children will attend this school, we have found another one already and they have been excepted there, hope fully you will find another Teacher in her place, or there will be more Parents who have something to say about her . Please send all the books and their things to our house , none of my children will stay here another minute . Motioning to Claudia, we all went out of his Office , now we where walking home when Claudia said , are we going to the new School tomorrow then Mom , may be first we have to go there, any way , to introduce you to the Teachers , at the same time we could take some of your things already over to the new house, we got the key , we might as well make use of it and bring some things there , on the weekend we get some help from some of the People dad is working with , come next Monday you go to the new School but for the next few days, it is nice to have you stay home with me, we can go to the Parks, or downtown and have a few nice days without school or work ,how is that ? In truth I had asked for a few days of at work which I got because we where moving in to the new place , that is one nice thing about this country here when one moves they do give you the time of specially if they know there are children involved . The Children where happy to hear about not going to School , for a few days of course , but for me it was nice too, we had not had time to really think about all of this ,the outlook to get in to a nice House made is forget some of the little things, but for the next day we went to the new School . It was a much nicer one than Balmoral , first of all because it was not right by the main Highway, second it had a very nice back yard that was fenced in to all sides, but off site from the Roads . Claudia liked it right away ,the boys where not to keen on it, but in time they would like it , since it was only ten minutes from home and they could come home for lunch every day . Everybody was very happy in the new House specially myself ,we had lots of room the boys as well as Claudia had their own rooms, now they could put up all their posters ,listen to their own music , no more , Mom, Joerg does not leave me alone ,or , Mom ,Dieter pushes my Lego house around ,that all was history, we had been thinking that from now on we should see to it that the boys did not have to share a room any more . We had been looking to build a House and found an area where we would like to live , it was just around the Mountain from where we lived then, but lucky for us ,we could take our time and one day we found a Builder who was in the exact area where we wanted to build . All went well our plans where good and the House to be a two story , where we had all the bed rooms upstairs and an extra bathroom as well . Any way ,life seemed to be very good to us , and two years later we where moving in to our new House . It was right on a Corner of a no thru road , there was hardly any traffic ,since we where one of the first ones moving in there , all the other houses where not finished yet , there was nobody on our street yet ,only down on the one corner of the main road there was one house finished,

People from Australia had moved in there . David, his wife and two boys, had moved in there , which was great, it gave our boys two other children to play with . Meanwhile I had started to work for Atco Industrial , a Company who builds Oil Camp Trailers , being the new Accounting Clerk , it was exciting work , I had studied for the past three years at night , to become that, it was not easy at times but now it was good ,getting this job was great for me, the money was excellent and all was well with the world . Two years after that , Peter came home one day just to tell me ,that he would be working for a Company in Kelwona British Columbia , " Western Star Trucks" they where called , well that was a shock to me . Okay we had been talking about moving one day to Kelowna , after having been there on a Holiday, but we did not want to move there now , specially since I got this great job . But , as faith would have it ,we moved after all , my great job was gone , in Kelowna ,there would not be another one like it , that was for sure , but my Husband believed, that it was not too hard to find a job like that in Kelowna . When we first got there he needed to go to the Company that had hired him, they had also paid for our move , but they had neglected to tell us that we had to look for a house on our own . Now that was a news flash , Peter had told me that they would have a house for us because I was not going to move there, if they had not done so, but he assured me that they did . There was no house for us , he did not have to start work for three more days there was a Holiday weekend in between , so we spend that looking around for a House . We found a very nice one too, where everybody had their own room again but it was a bit out of the way for the children, for me it was okay getting on the bus would be okay since we only had one car at that time .

From then on we started to have problems with Claudia and Dieter but mostly Claudia , she believed that we had done this move on purpose, to hurt her feelings , because she had to leave her friends behind . Understanding to a point what she was trying to tell us, but on the other hand we are six people who are involved in this, I told her not just you , the boys seem to be okay with this, even so they had to leave their friends behind as well, but they can come to visit . Remember, most of them come here any way in the Summer Holidays , see , Kelowna was more of a Holiday resort ,for most people, there was the Okanagan Lake, a very big one at that , and in the summer time there where thousands of people here from all over the country ,specially from Calgary, we had been here twice when we lived in Calgary . But for my daughter this was hell , she needed to take the Transit bus, which was understood only would run up to where we lived twice a day at that time , it was either that or to walk to the Mall, which was about six miles from where we lived .

My Husband being typical German Male believed it would build character if the children would learn how to walk a few miles ,but that was very unrealistic , where my own opinion was concerned ,to walk all that way none of their friends would make that journey and for me , knowing that my children would have to walk alongside a busy Highway was not okay , it was always a point of argument between my Husband and myself . Neither one of us wanted anything to happen to the kids ,so most at the time it was me who would drive them down to where ever they wanted to go, or we all walked , or took the bus, only on certain days and my Husband would pick us up going home, because his office was right across from the Mall . It was a very difficult time for me , knowing that my children should walk , where there was no side walk made me shudder, what if with all those cars who where driving like there was no tomorrow , something would happen to one of them, or all three of them when they walked that way . So beginning to scout out that area , I started to walk when they went to School , just to find a better way to walk , and there was one ! Only half a mile down the road there was a small Country Road who lead right down through some of the Orchards who where along side that road , and ended up on the main road, leading to the Mall, but at least the last two miles. When one came out on to that road there was a side walk, not a real one but enough space for People to go on the side , not on the road . Besides that , being much shorter than the highway , it was also very nice to go that way ,almost no cars would drive there because of the road being so narrow , and all the fruit trees where so nice to look at most at the time . One day while walking there , a Tractor came and needed to cross the road where I was walking to go down town , the Farmer asked me where I was from , well actually from Germany ,but we live here now and had lived in Calgary for eight years , would you like to pick fruit or have you ever picked any , no not really , in Calgary there ,are no fruit trees with the Winter being what it is and there is no spring time really only winter and summer ,but other than that nothing . Have you ever, picked , Apples ,or Pears or Cherries , yes back home with my Dad but that was a long , long time ago , may be this is different now . When is the season for that , asking him, he told me that in about two weeks they would start picking cherries , after that Plums than Apples and so on , the season goes right in to the Winter time because the Pears as well as some kinds of Apples are picked very late in the year . Turning , to go down the hill , he said , may be you could think about it, come down if you have time in about two weeks okay ? Just might do that , having said that, turned around and walked away , since I had no job here , it might be nice to work in an Orchard . Walking along picturing my self picking cherries , that would not be such a bad idea , may be we could get some to take home, after all, the children would love to have some . That was my biggest problem , in all the years of raising my children , every time there was any new development , the children where the once that came first, never thinking of my self or my Husband, only my four sweeties . Any way , arriving at the Mall walking around inside it took me to the south side where the Phones where , if I did not want to walk all the way back up to the House my Husband should know that he had to come at lunch time to bring me home ,for him with the car it was only five to ten minutes but for me to walk it would be half an hour . Which was not to bad the only thing is that when one had cleaned the house since six in the morning than walked six miles one is very tired already but than when it came to the afternoon there was the cooking to be done for everybody that was no small task either . But cooking was one of my favorite things , if phoning my husband one never knew if he was in a good mood, most at the time he was not , that had to do with his job here . He had been promised so many things by that company but never any of them had been kept, now he was there and did not want to quit, since the pay was not the best ,but it helped us to live there besides, I would go to work as soon as we had settled in fully . For now he was the only one who earned Money and he was not very happy . But he was today , lucky for me, because he had gotten a promotion finally , the one who he was supposed to get when he started, but never the less , he got it and his mood was such that he did not mind at all to bring me home ,as a matter of fact he asked me out to lunch that day, which was very nice . Telling him over lunch my encounter with the Farmer up on the Mountain side , that is not such a bad idea to go and pick fruit he said , how much are they paying ? Well I do not know that since not being in the market to be a picker ,it never occurred to me to ask that question . You should go and find out my husband said, may be it is good pay and we can get some fruit for cheaper , than in the stores . Always looking for a bargain , one has to do that in order to make ends meet, but we did a good job of that ,the children always had enough food clean clothes and lots of love given to them . Sometimes when I was alone at home I got very angry at God , telling him that it would be very nice if my Mom & Dad would still be here so they could tell me if I did everything right . Other times , I was just mad that there was nobody there for me to talk to , it was not easy raising four children having nobody to ask or talk to , at times it was very hard, believe me and those times God was so far away from me , that's what I thought . After one of those days where nothing was right for me , my Daughter had given me a hard time, my oldest son was going out to a Friend we did not know , it was not one of my best days that was for sure, but that night my Husband got scared for me , in the middle of the night I let out a scream that woke him and the boys up since they where on the same floor as we where . The Dream was about my Mother , she had been on my mind for several weeks now and that day talking to her in my mind was not so good because now blaming her for not being there for me . Any way , my Husband wanted to know what happened so did the two older boys .Dreaming about my mom was not a surprise, often did I have the same dream , my Mom was walking with me towards the Train Station, when she got on the train she always said to me , we see each other soon okay , give my love to the children and remember , I do love you very much . This time when she got on the train she did not say that, but instead this ," now my sweet you can do this , it will be the last time that we talk ,I wont be coming back any more . While she was getting on the train I could see my Dad waving at me through the window , than they both stood at that window and waved at me good by . Hearing my self crying out , you can not do that , you have to come back I need to see you and talk to you again ! But she did not look out any more , when the train left the Station I was still standing there crying telling her to come back ,when all of a sudden, this very bright light came towards me , the train had gone out of my sight around the corner, but this light was coming very fast , trying to turn back I could not move , when I heard this voice ," you have to let go of her now , there is nothing she can do for you any more ,after all you are a grown up , behave like one , she loves you and will always be close by, just look in your heart she will be there . Sweat was running down my forehead as I woke up sitting upright in my bed, my Husband telling me to stop crying . You are scaring all of us he said , please what was wrong . For a few minutes, catching my breath was hard because I felt like I could not breathe , after a while , was able to tell my family what had happened , all but the part where this light came towards me but my husband could tell there was something else, so he kept asking me about it . Well yes there was this very scary light , the air seemed to leave me I could not catch my breath , it was so powerful that it scared me , that must have woken me up ! May be , now you can leave your Mom to rest, she deserves that don't you think. . Yes that could be, but I still miss her a lot ,when there is no one else to talk to, she was there for me, but since she had died there was no other person I trusted with any thing that needed to be said . Understand one thing, he said , she deserves to be happy ,now you saw your dad with her , they are together now again, and very glad to be that way, they both deserve to be left alone now okay ? Well if any one else had said that to me the answer would have been no , but my Husband who had gone through so much with me, he knew what was best for all of us and that was , I needed to let go of my Mother , since she had died, that had not happened ,but now it was time, after all she had been gone for fifteen years already, but it seemed to me as if it was yesterday . Like my Dad told me one time , the pain will get less but never go away, he was right , it never did go away, not even today ,after almost forty years . After that night there was a change in me , not only did the anger go away but also I found my self looking to me , when there was something to be done, or figured out , it was not my Mom that I talked to any more , well sometimes it still was, but not in an angry state, but always full of love . It is funny how some things go with me, this was the way of God telling me to let go of my mother, that she deserved to be happy and well as she was now . A few years after that , we had just moved to another House we had bought , a log home which my husband loved to get , this was not a big move , it was still in the same town ,just on the opposite end from town . Up on a steep hill where no bus was going , now I needed to take Joerg and Dieter to Scholl as well as Peter junior but only for the first year, after that they had School buses going for them, but for one year I lived out of my car so to speak . My two older sons had both gotten a job in a Restaurant ,where the owner was from Germany , both he and his wife where good people ,they offered me a job as well just to help out for a while because they could not find good help, but that job was okay . The only thing was I needed to start at six in the morning, than pick up junior from school bring him to the Restaurant so he could have some lunch and after three o'clock went home with him . Dieter and Joerg needed to be picked up after ten at night but sometimes they had sports and in between job and driving them everywhere there was no time to think, really ,but in the car I would still talk to my Mom ,also to God , but I was very careful what or how that talk would go . Another night like the one that time, would not be too good, so very carefully selecting my words was telling my mom how this all is going to get to me , this is too much I told her , there is never any time for rest or to do something for my self . One time she told me that I should not pay to much attention to me , it is more important that your children are okay , that they are happy and healthy , you are not one of the most important people on earth ,do you know that she said . Of course, that was not what I wanted to hear, but it was okay ,she was right and from then on there was no more complains from my side . A few more years went by Joerg was graduating already , Dieter never did , he quit School three months before graduation, that was a blow to us , he had so much potential he was smart good looking very nice character but all of that went out the window in just a few weeks . To my Husband and my self , it was very hard to understand what was going on ,but Joerg told us that Dieter wanted to have his own life, make his own choices , haven't we let you all do that so far , any one of you has been able to develop your own identity what now . Asking my Husband , why this would have happened, he only said that may be Dieter got in with the wrong crowd and now did not listen to anything we had to say any more . This is not good , and talking to my Son Dieter did not help either, he was very stubborn , there was only one thing to do , talk to God , he knew what was going on he was the one and only who could put a stop to all of that nonsense, but he did not . As much as I prayed there was not help insight , Dieter still did his own thing and one day just left home without telling us he would go , we found out when we got home , he had left a note telling us not to come and look for him ,but that he was with his friend and they both would go and work in Calgary . Everybody was very stunned , we could not believe that he had gone and done this, my heart was breaking for fear that he might not be okay , but than one day I just broke down , crying so much was not good for me either but there was my last prayer for Dieter , please God help him , look after him and keep your hand over him, protect him from harm ,and bring him home save I pray in Jesus name , Amen . It took me a while to come to grips with the fact, that one of my kids was out there alone , but my best Friend Helga was in Calgary , writing to here telling her what happened was the first thing I did after finding Dieters note ,phoning her would be easier but it would have taken an hour to explain why he left home because for my self and my husband we had no idea that he would do this . Naturally my friend told me that if she heard from him she would let me know , also that she would try to talk some sense in to him about coming home again . After about two weeks of being in such a state that I started to cry whenever someone mentioned my sons name , we got a call from my friend, from Calgary , she told us that Dieter had been at her house with his friend , both of them looked okay to her but she gave them some food anyway , to take to their apartment ,they both had gotten a job at one of the Restaurants in town and where doing okay . Now that was good news , that night for the first time I slept all the way through , but only for one night because a week after that she phoned me telling me that they where not at the apartment any more , she had gone there to bring them some more food, but was told by the Landlord that they had been kicked out a week ago because they could not pay the rent they only had given him the deposit for the first month but after that nothing . Helga then went to the Restaurant that they had told her about , only to find out that they never worked there in the first place . Having heard all of this it did not do me any good, by going there myself , where would I start looking , talking to God was the only thing to do, he truly was the one and only who could keep my son from coming to any harm, and bring him home to us . It was a very hard time for all of us , but specially for Joerg and Peter junior, the both of them where right there seeing me cry all the time for fear something might happen to my child , but than one night another dream came to me why . Heaven only knows ,but it was good, walking down the road ,which was nothing special , we had done that so many times my children and I, but this time it was special because my Dad came towards me , he was dressed in the special blue Suite that I had bought for him many years ago while working in a Textile Factory , he smiled as he reached out to take my hand in to his . Why are you in such a state , have you not left home when you where his age , did you not find another person to share your life with when you where his age ? What is wrong about him going out on his own , why are you making such a fuss about that ? Still smiling , holding on to my hands , look he said , you know that God works in very funny ways sometimes , which we often do not understand ,but we have to be okay with them because , he does know best , he will keep Dieter save, do not worry about that ,but he also will teach your son a lesson . Hopefully he can learn from it , if not ,than that is something Dieter has to deal with ,not you , let go of him , he still is your son ,but he does not have to be by your side at all times , those days are over ! Giving my Dad a big hug felt so good , telling him that from now on I would try to have more confident in God and not take all the world on my self . That is a good Girl he said , and it sounded funny because in all the years when growing up , my dad had never called me a Girl , he always called me his Jungens , It was done out of affection for me because being the last one of ten children I was home the longest and always had a lot of respect for my parents, because they let me become my own person, not telling me always what to do or not to do ,. When a mistake was made, it was my mistake and it needed to be that way , only then one can learn something about life . Come morning it was clear to me that God had send my Dad to let me know that I needed to let my son make his own mistakes ,or he would not learn anything, I also tried not to think about him, being out there to much , if God can look after him there was nothing to worry about besides , he was the one who promised me that if I believe in him and his son , that anything I wished would be done , may be not everything , but most of them, and up to now he always fulfilled his promise to me . One thing puzzled me after all , how could my son go to Calgary , not having a lot of Money because he left without any money , his pay day was not before two weeks after he had left and Arno which was his Boss at the time gave that envelope to Joerg who than brought it home . This was one child one could always count on , so I thought , Joerg ,who never got to upset or did not show it too much, if he did get upset , but he always had an explanation for most things and yet he was only eighteen , but he had found a Girl who he loved as he told me . Some Parents ,would say this is to early to have a Girl friend but at eighteen, he was almost more grown up than some thirty year olds . Having just finished High School and looking for a job he knew what he wanted but he was one of my children who would badly disappoint me a lot of times , not because he would do something stupid ,but because he listened to the wrong People . This is what happened , he met this Girl her name was Marnie she had a younger sister by the name of Michelle , one day he told me that he had fallen in love with Michelle while at their House , where Marnie had invited him . He had guts ,we have to give him that, because he went straight to Michelle's Father telling him how he felt and that he would like to Marry his youngest Daughter . Now at that time , Michelle was only sixteen years old, but her Father told Joerg that ,if he could wait till her eighteen Birthday, he would give his okay for him to Marry her . When my son came home and told us we where very happy for him, but a voice in the back of my head told me that there was something not quite right , but I could not put my finger on it, so I let it slide . For all I knew it might be okay, after all, who knew everything, certainly not me ,but my gut feeling told me that my sons future Father in law would give us some grieve and he did ,a lot of it ! First of all he gave my son Money to buy his first house, he had to make a lot of repairs but the end result was a very nice house, which made my son think that he was better now than his Parents , at least much better than his Mother, by not coming home any more but getting a rented place . To his excuse I have to say that ,we had to go to Germany for about one year ,he could have stayed in the house ,but he did not want to, understandable to a point,, since that house was to far away for him to be getting to his Girlfriends place . His future Mother in law helped him to find a rental place from which he then repaired the house he had bought ,with the Money Mr. Willms had lend him for two years , but when he sold the house he gave the money back of course. From then on, it was even worst . When we came back from Germany we had nothing any more , only all our things that we had put in storage in Kelowna , the house was sold while we had been gone, but we found another one, very nice one , that was for Rent with option to buy after two years . Looking down from that house on to the Okanagan Lake across the other side we saw the Mountains, it was a great location , but for my son it was still not good enough , he always asked us if we would not build a house bigger and better than this one . Telling him time and time again that we are very happy, where we lived he did not come quit that often any more just once in a while leaving Peter junior behind ,where he used to come to go to the pictures with him, once in a while ,now he did not come at all any more, the only times he would come if he had something to tell us about his new in laws . At his Wedding we where not permitted to sit at the head table because we where not considered proper People , we had not as much money as the Willms Family had , our house was not as big as theirs was, besides , we did not belong to their Church, which I thought was a blessing, because by their behavior , they where not good Christians , from what I knew about the Bible , and that is a lot since my Mother thought me about that book, as soon as I could speak , honestly , those people where not good Christian People . Any body who believes they are better than the next guy has not an inkling about the Bible , God tells all of us who are reading his book that we are all alike in his eyes, nobody is better or worst , specially not if one does not have as much money as the next guy, but for the Willms that was enough to push us aside . When they had any parties or family get together as they called it ,we where never invited why , one can only guess . But when it came that they needed us to help them out with something they would call and ask us to come over to help with picking fruit . At the time they did have an Orchard and since they did not want to ,pay anybody for picking , they always asked their own Family members or us . We did help, because being a good reader of the bible I also know , when asked for help never say no ,if you can help , my mother had raised me that way too, so to me, it was only natural that I would help . My Husband did not want anything to do with them any more, because he had heard some stories that Michelle and her Mother had been telling around town . Kelowna was a small place when we first lived there most people knew one another, there was not much that would go by someone , so needless to say ,even I had been told a lot of stories that they had been telling . But for myself , my mother also had told me, never to listen to gossip , of course some of the things that where said where thru like I found out one day . Michelle's Aunt who I met in the Mall one day , wanted me to sit down with her for a cup of coffee , she was very nice and there was no reason not to do so . After a while we started talking and she asked me if we had been mad at Joerg for not having us sit at his table on his Wedding day .No we where not , but it was not very nice of him to do this to us, but he had his reasons we where sure of that, and today was the day I would find out what they had been , those reasons . First of all was the fact that we did not pay for the wedding ,but as much as we knew , when a Daughter gets Married the parents pay for the wedding, but when a son gets Married , his parents have to pay for the wedding . Michelle was the second Daughter of Bert and Christine Willms ,they had only Marnie ,the older one of the girls, she was not Married yet but as it turned out she had been in love with my son as well . Not to go in to the whole dramatic of that relationship, but it was not very good, to this day it is not one hundred percent ,between the two sisters . It is not my place to go in to those kind of things, but praying a lot was the best part of my life in those days ,because with God I did not have to be afraid to speak my mind ,where with my son Joerg, we always had to be very careful what we said, he did not like any negative words to be spoken by us ,but he would say things like , well Mom you could get a better car, don't you think, or , why cant you get some nicer clothes to wear . He would always make jokes about us in front of his in laws , even his father in law could do nothing else but insult us every time we got together, which by the way was not at their house ,but at ours . For a number of years I would have one Sunday of every month where I would give a big Brunch ,for which my two sons would be invited as well as their in laws , his sister in law Marnie which never showed up once in seven years , she thought she could not stand the fact that we lived in a small house, and we did not have the money she had or her Father had ,because both Girls lived off their Parents still, they got a job at their fathers business and their Husbands got one there to . Thinking about that now it was strange how Bert Willms held on to all of them with a tight rope, like we say , but he truly did . Not one of them would have a job if not for him, because they had not a very good education but since it was a family business they all worked there even his Wife sometimes . That was okay with me, we had not too much to do with them unless they would come to our Brunches, we never saw them other wise . Then after four years being married they got their first child , a little girl by the name of Haley , we had not been told of her birth until two days after she had been born ,only then where we permitted to come and see her . For the longest time I would look after Haley every Monday , which was my day with her and I took this day of from work since I had my own business as a Janitorial kind it was easy to take that time of to spend with my favorite girl ,the baby would be at my house all day , it gave Michelle a day of and also a chance to go and do some shopping that she could not do other wise . When my children where small they where always with me no matter where I went , my kids where too . But I guess now in these times, the young mothers can not do what we used to have to do , look after our own children ,only once in a while would my best friend baby sit with my three children actually only three times in all those years . Never mind that ,but than Haley would say something about her other Grandma or Grandpa, she could not talk very good but she told me that they had said , she Haley would go to see her crazy Grandma , which hurt my feelings very much, but I never said anything to either my son or his wife, because it would have meant not to have the pleasure of seeing my baby every Monday and they all knew that . This went on for all the years we lived there ,every time my sweetie was at my house I heard a new saying that she had been told by them ,she always said , but I love you Oma , that was what she called me, because she told me she loved me so much , because I never said anything bad about the other Grandparents . To this day, I am very glad that I did not . We moved away , now seven years to the day from Kelowna, we bought a nice house with almost six acres, but the funny part was this . As we had moved in but not quit settled I got a phone call from Michelle's Mother, she wanted to know if I was coming to Kelowna to visit with the children, it had only been five months since we had moved here and we had not fully settled in, but telling her that I might be coming for Haley's Birthday, which was the end of August . Now that was okay with her but then came the funniest question any body ever asked me to this day ,I do not believe to this day that she had the gall to ask me this , " could you please bring the Mortgage Agreement we would like to see if you truly bought the house on an acreage ! Nearly falling of my chair at the time ,but telling her that if I would come , it was not going to be to show her what kind of Mortgage we had ,or needed to pay every month, that was none of her business . Hang up ,on her, thinking that God had a good sense of humor where I was concerned , when another call came in the next day from my son Joerg . He was not coming right out what he wanted , but in the end he finally came out with ," can you bring the Mortgage Papers Mom, I would like to see how much you had to pay for an acre ,we would like to by an acreage too ,but do not know how much it would cost us . That was a very dumb thing to ask me , knowing that his in laws had put him up to this . He goes to Church every Sunday but can't be honest about anything any more ,the whole Family is like that , Drama Queens, and liars it is very sad . Growing up like I had, my Mother was Jewish decent my Father Catholic, it was no wonder that we knew so much about the Bible , both of my Parents thought us about their old Family Bibles , it was very interesting to learn about Mother Mary , on the other hand it was great to learn how Jesus was Gods only Son born by Mary who had a Husband named Josef . When growing up a lot of People named their Son Josef and their Daughter Mary , it was like Peter and Paul ,the two Men who followed Jesus where ever he went . But there never was a controversial conflict in my Family, because of the two Religions, as a matter of fact , we learned about the Jewish Religion more than may of the Jewish People, and yet, my Mother was third generation Jewish on her great Grandfathers side . When I was going to the Lutheran Church , it was okay with both my Parents ,they left it up to us Children to decide which believe we would choose for ourselves , as long as we believed that God, was the one and only ,there was no other . Some different Countries might have other beings they call their God but in reality there is only one God , we all know that, but to this day the Jewish People will not believe that Jesus is the son of God , and because of that ,they will never be able to live in peace , until they do ,that is what my mother told us over and over again growing up .She insisted that if the Jewish People ever say yes to Jesus ,they will have peace, but as long as they don't they will not . She believed that with all her Heart and so do I , the Bible tells us that if we believe God will give us everything we ask him for , now that is a very big thing to say ,because I do believe that he does not give us everything, but only because it is in our best interest that we do not get all we ask for , he knows what we need and that ,we will have always ,but some of the items we would ask for we do not get . But that does not mean he is not listening , he is all the time , let me just tell a few instances where I needed him desperately and he was there for me, if you read on you know why for me believing in him is very easy !

One time when we needed some extra money , my children needed some new clothes and we wanted to buy some new Living room furniture we where still living in Germany , my oldest sister came by and told me that I could help out at the big October fest kind of Celebration in the next town ,they where looking for people who would carry all those Beer Jugs . Now since I had never done that kind of work, but wanted to make some money , said yes, and next day my Sister went with me to this Guy who owned a Hotel in the next town, he was the one who had put up a huge Tent for about two hundred and fifty people .There where all long tables each one seating about twenty People .

Shortly before the first Guests where arriving, the Owner called us to the front ,just to let us know that two of the girls would not be coming, instead we needed to serve more people each than first anticipated ! Well that was not to good , but thinking that if God gave me that chance, he would let me do this job as best I could . Sure enough my Sister & I made a lot of money that weekend , about five hundred Deutsch mark every night . The tips where all ours too, it was great we had enough to buy the furniture and enough clothes for the children after that weekend . But the down side was that ,the Owner had called my sister on the phone, asking her to meet him at a Restaurant and to bring me with her , now that was very strange to me, but since he had been so nice to let me work there for him I did not want to disappoint my sister either, so we both went . Not knowing that it was a set up between my sister and him, he wanted me to sit right next to him, while my sister excused herself told me she needed to go to the Lady's room ,but never came back . After a while it dawned on me , that this was not going to be a meeting where we would find out if we could work again for this Guy , he was making it very clear to me what he wanted . Pretending to have to go where my sister went ,telling him that I would be right back ,walked to the Hallway where the Restrooms where, but than saw a back door open, to which the escape was perfect ,but my car was gone . My sister who had asked me if she could drive to the meeting , had kept the key and gone home without me ,how dirty was that . Feeling kind of lost, this had never happened to me before in all my life , tears where going to run down my face ,but than knowing that his promise goes for me too ,asked him for help, but while running towards the next bus stop realized , the only thing was, I could not stand out there, he would spot me right away if he came after me, so there was another Pub, about twenty paces in front of me right behind the bus stop. That would be it, thinking out loud to myself, went in there only to hear from the Girl who was behind the counter, "we are closed you have to come back tomorrow. Please let me hide here, someone is following me, "okay go right through here and stay down under one of the tables, since it is dark in there nobody can see you there, but what if the guy comes in here ? Not to worry she said, we have someone in the back room who is doing some cleaning up, he is a strong guy, but whoever is going to come looking for you, he wont find you ,I promise. She said that so convincing that I believed her, and went to hide in the next room, not sooner had I sat down behind one big table when I could hear a door open, this Guy came in there and by his voice could hear that he was very mad at me. Asking the Girl ," did a young Woman just come in here ?" No sorry she said, we are closed today, there is nobody here, but tomorrow we will be open if you like to come back then. No ,that is not what I had in mind he said, but he came towards the room where I was hiding, but never saw me. The whole time hiding under there I was praying that God would let me get home okay, everything else was not important right now ,but as for my sister she would get an ear full, besides that, she would never get my car, ever again, nor would I go work with her any where any more. Hearing the Guy leave but still sitting there waiting for the Girl in front to come and get me, she came a few minutes later calling me to come out of hiding, he is gone I even looked outside he is not there any where. Can I do anything else for you she asked ," yes may be, could you phone my Friend to pick me up, my sister took my car, there is no bus going any more . Of course ,please follow me , showing me where the phone was , she went to the front just to make sure that this guy would not return for me, I had to phone to my friend myself . . He did not come back in there again , and my best friend Franzy came to pick me up, she was very upset when she was told what had happened ,she had been sitting with my children and had to get her mom to take over for her while she was coming to get me . You see , God, was there for me, so that no harm would come to me , he made his presents felt by me because there was no fear any more like the first few minutes when I was running over to the next Pub ,besides that , the pub I was hiding in was never open on Mondays meaning that the doors where always looked the Girl told me so herself she could not explain why the door had been open that day , but I could . Another story was even worst , one day my Girl friend and I had decided to go out for an hour or so in to one of the nice discos we got in those days , her mother would stay at my house with the children and we could go out ,since we had not been out for a long time this felt nice , just the two of us , going in to this nice place ,we sat down and started talking about the past few weeks, when all of a sudden, someone pulling me by my arm, up from my chair , it was the same guy that had been stood up by me about two months ago , what was he doing here , all the other times we had come here he had never been there besides , he was married and had five children , that much I knew, what did he want from me ? Now that hurts, I was telling him, than looking around for someone who could help me, because Franzy was just small just like me ,we did not have the strength to fend of this crazy guy , he was determent to take me outside with him , the last minute I yelled out , Help , when a few guys saw him pulling me towards the door ,two of them came over . Where are you going with this Lady ,one asked him , that is none of your business he said , but now I pulled away from him ,he was concentrating on the two guys , not paying to much attention to me at that moment , but running over to my friend , sitting down we let the two Men handle him, they went outside with him , but he never came back inside . Thinking that he had enough now and he would leave me alone , one of the Men who helped me came over , we found out that one of the men who had helped me knew me ,because of my brother Helmut , you know he said, what did he want with you , telling him the whole story about what my sister did to me , he shock his head . He is married you know , I said , he has a very nice wife and five kids I never did anything , for him to come after me, I hardly knew him ,only because by working there for the weekend that was all . Well , he wont be coming in here any more ,we told him if he did he would have to deal with the two of us, my other bouncer who helped you . That is very kind of you, we do not go out to much ,but once in a while we like to come here, because nobody bothers us here, we can dance with any body without having them ask us to go home with them, you know what I mean ? Oh yes, I do he said , but you should tell your brother about this guy , no, that wont be necessary, he probably has enough now that he found out we got some help . But I was mistaken, that guy did not give up, he must be truly crazy, my friend said to me , it was my day for driving , we changed, one time it was my car, the next it was her car , but today it was mine ,. Having a BMW which was a fast car, sometimes may be to fast for my own good ,but tonight it would serve me very well , we had gotten in to our car and started driving off when looking in the rear view mirror could see another car , that car I knew , Franzy, that crazy guy is behind us , he must have waited all this time just to get to us , what can we do ? Right now there is nothing we can do , just drive , praying to myself asking God for guidance ,how to handle this , please God tell me what to do let us get home okay, do not let this Man drive us of the road . Knowing that his answer would come, my first being scared did not last too long . We had to go on the Highway just for twenty minutes, and that would be my time when we could loose him , talking to my friend about that ,we where sure that he would not follow us , but we needed him to go past us , pulling over just before going on to the Highway ramp, he had to pass us because there was another care behind him , seeing him go by letting the other car go too we pulled in right behind the both of them . Driving as usual pretty fast , he slowed down , may be he believed we would pass him by ,but we did not , slowing down my self , he went a bit faster, now was my chance ,we stayed right on his tail , it was dangerous but it was the only way we could get rid of him , by staying right on him he needed to go faster ,but in about five minutes our turn off from the Highway would be in sight and we had to get off there. That's what we where counting on, him going a bit faster ,I pretended to go faster too ,by staying right behind him waving, as to let him know we would follow him . Making him believe that he had won and I would come right after him where ever he wanted to go ,but as soon as he passed the turn off hitting the brake turning the wheel praying to God that my Car would not make a U turn but stay in its tracks , and it did , some other car would probably have tipped over, but not this one . We went home laughing about the stunt we pulled on him , you better tell your brother about this guy he might go and have a talk to him. No there is a better way that he would leave me alone, and that is the way I choose to go. As soon as we got home I phoned his Wife, knowing it was very late in the day but she was up, since they had a Hotel she was probably up all the time late. Telling her all about his behavior towards me ,also letting her know that I had no intentions of going out with him, or anything else for that matter, and would she please see to it that he left me alone? That was all we had to do, so we thought but a few weeks later as the kids and myself where at Franziskas House the door bell rang, now she lived on the third floor of a Apartment building at that time, her Mother was there and her sister, we all had the children with us they where playing nicely in the other room while we where in the living room. When she opened the door this guy was standing in front of her yelling to see me, how he ever knew where I was with my children, we did not know at that time, but then we found out very fast, my dear sister had told him where, he was yelling wanting to see me , we had some issues to clear up he said, as I was walking towards the front door Franziskas Mother beat me too it almost ,but he could see me. Meanwhile the sister of my friend was calling for the Police, this guy was truly crazy and we had thought that he would leave me alone, but now we found out why he did not. Your Sister had told me that you would go to bed with me he said, my face turned white as a sheet, please say that again, yes she did tell me that you liked me very much ,and would like to go out with me. That was not the truth, believe me, there was never any mentioning about you and me ever ,the only thing that I wanted to do was, making some extra money by working for you there, on that weekend, never did I say anything about you and,

me never ! Having three children I do not have very much time for anything else, but them , and cleaning my house , at night I work for the Textile Factory ,so there is never enough time for myself let alone for anybody else . Why did you phone my wife then , because , you did not leave me alone, and that was the only way to get you to stop this coming after me . Even had told my brothers about you they had been on the look out for you , this is hopefully the last time we meet .Sorry , if I scared you ,but that was not my intention ,all that I wanted was to go out with you after your sister had told me about you know what, never did I think for a moment that it could not be thru, but now it is okay you wont hear about me any more promise !

    That would be great ,because as everybody knows, you have five children and a lovely wife , you should not be doing this kind of thing honestly . Well you might be right but thinking about what your sister told me, it was an easy way to get you to go out with me ,sorry again and please forgive me . The Police had arrived and was coming up the Stair way , has anybody of you phoned us, the one Officer asked , yes we did , my girlfriend told him, but we had already straightened this whole thing out with this Gentlemen , he apologized and all is okay !

No need for us then to stick around is there , no, not really ,telling the one Officer what it had been all about he looked at the guy, than over to me smiling to me he said , now for a bit I can understand why he would like to go out with you ,but since you told me that he is married he should stay home with his Family ,not run after you right ? May be it was all a misunderstanding my Girlfriend said to him , her sister had told this Man that she would go out with him , pointing at me she said , but my friend does not go out unless I am with her and my Daughter and her Husband , other than that we do not go out ,most at the time we stay home, like tonight , we have some people in and celebrate, that way we can have our children right here with us . After they all had left it was time for me to go home too with the children, they where quiet tired already, and work was waiting for me . There are some very strange things , I need to let everybody know about ,this next one was a bit scary but never the less it was all because of God , I do believe that with all my Heart , he was telling me something . We had just moved up to the Mountain side on an Acreage , just finished unpacking all of the things ,putting them in to their places ,when, while walking outside to see what all needed to be done out there I saw some Coyotes ,now never had there been anything about those kind of Animals written that said they would attack a person, so much was known to me, but it was scary to see them up close ,any way . Off to the side of the house someone had made a bit of a Garden , but it had been overgrown with weeds , since I love gardening, decided to make a new one with just a few vegetables for us. The following day, I was out there cleaning up the weeds and finding that there was still some little vegetable growing ,it looked like carrots or something but it was not ,pulling it out, made good sense to me, since needing the whole space for the once I wanted to plant there . While working for a while there was a funny sound , looking up there where the Coyotes again, this time there where four of them, about twenty feet away from me , but between the House and myself there was no way that I could run anywhere, if they decided to attack me, so we just all stood there watching each other for the longest time . My Heart was pounding like crazy , not knowing what to do , but then starting to walk towards them, but it only looked that way probably to them ,because , the house was where my steps wanted to take me, but since they stood in between there ,it must have looked to them that I was coming towards them . Lucky for me that I had that rake in my hand , they must have thought it was a gun or so ,but they walked backwards keeping their eyes still on me . We had no dog then, but that might have been lucky for the dog, because as we heard later that some of those Coyotes had killed dogs too . Not knowing if they would be out there again I stayed in the house, until my Sons got home from School , than the three of us walked around outside to see if they would be still there ,but telling my husband that the Garden would have to wait until we could be sure those animals where gone . The whole day thinking about what they wanted from me, those Coyotes, they just stood there watching me but did not come any closer, it was strange . The dream that night was no less frightening , as working out in my Garden , the Coyotes came back ,but this time they where coming closer and closer towards me, they could not have been more than four feet away from me when all of a sudden, one of them was flying through the air , than the next one ,and the next one , looking around me there where my two brothers , my dad , my Mom and my Sister, who had all died years before, but they where throwing them away from me , my oldest Brother Harry came over to were I was standing telling me , you never have to be afraid any more , we are all here to look out for you, nobody will harm you believe that . Naturally , all I wanted was , to talk to all of them ,not realizing that it was a dream , but the next morning, the feeling of fear was gone , when going out to my garden there was no more fear, the coyotes where still up on the hill looking down on me, but they did not come closer any more . That was one of the scary happenings , at the same time also a happy one , I got to see my Mom ,Dad and Brothers and my one Sister who had passed away just six month before . A lot of people say that this is just wishful thinking, and may be it is for some of them, but to me ,this was one of Gods messages, to let me know that there was no need to be afraid ,he had a team of Angels around me, my own team , which to this day have kept me save from any harm . My Husband being an Engineer, was called to go to the United States , to work there for a few years , now we had been there many times on Holidays along the Oregon Coast but never thought we would be living there . It would be a great opportunity for my Husband, as an Engineer, but for me it was like someone had just taken my favorite toys away, and put me in a dark closet . Moving would mean , to have to leave my children behind, all of them, not only that ,but my two little Granddaughters who I loved so very much ! There was no way that we could see each other once or twice a week , up to now , they had been at my house once a week ,for the whole day, it was always the best day of the week for me, never would I have believed anybody, who told me that one could love two Girls as much as I loved those two . Specially Haley, she not only had the comets name , to me she was the comet , Haley, she came in to my life and that was it , she had my Heart my soul everything, she was such a great baby and is now a young lady, who anybody has to love, if they wanted to or not . The same goes for Georgia , she is such a sweetie , a gentle little girl ,always having a lot of questions ,she reminds me of myself a lot , always having so much questions for my parents . Thinking of having to leave those girls behind , my heart was breaking in thousand pieces, I could just feel it , the bottom had gone out under my feet . But also knowing that this would be the best thing for my Husband , it was one of the toughest choices that I had to make in all my life . Asking God for help was natural for me , since he is the one who sends us where ever he wants us to be , he was the only one who knew my pain too ,but this time it seemed that the answer had to be my own ,he did not help in any way , at least not at first, and so it was that every night crying myself to sleep was the norm . That went on for about two weeks ,we had to pack everything ,the Company was paying for the move to the States , the big Truck was sitting in front of the House already for half a day ,there was so much to do that last day .There was no time to think . My Son Joerg had phoned me, to tell me that they had a last dinner prepared for us that afternoon ,the Carpet cleaner did not come at the right time, he was two hours late . Having to do the whole House it took him three hours, which made us late for my sons dinner, but it was okay, they all had been a bit late , he was not home in time from work either , Michelle my daughter in law had not gotten home from work on time so it was okay, just the way things turn out sometimes . What we did not know was that my oldest Son Dieter ,would be there to with his two sons, and his wife . Having had so much to do the past few days , that day was the worst of my life , seeing the children play, knowing that I would not be here for a while to see them like this , looking at my Haley and Georgia they had a sad expression on their little faces, but gave me a big smile any way . Haley asking me , Oma when are you coming back to us , why do you have to go too , Opa can go alone and come home on the weekends . It was hard to explain to the children why we had to move , and the reason that I was going to , we are a team Opa & Oma ,I said , and where ever one goes the other one does to, it is the way that God wants it to be, as soon as one gets Married, this is the way, ask your Mom & Dad about this they can tell you . Which did not make it any easier for anybody, but it helped a bit , all through dinner nobody said anything about the move, the subject was not a favorite with anybody right now . After the dinner we had to leave and the good bys where so hard on everyone , a smile was hurting my face because my heart was telling me to cry, but in face of all my children I wanted to be brave, and not cry ,they should be happy to know that their Mother and Grandmother would have a good life in the States too ,just like here ,only she would miss her children very much .Our last night was spend in a Hotel the house was cleaned up the Realtor would be there next morning to put up the for sale sign, we did not want to be there any more, it was so empty, even our dog did not want to go in to the house any more . That night the dream was about my Father again , as I was going shopping , in my dream , going around one corner where the road would go a bit uphill , he was coming down towards me . At first ,I did not recognize him , he looked so tall with his dark blue suit , he smiled at me and asked me to sit down with him for a Coffee, funny enough ,always in those dreams I am the only one who is having a coffee , but never the less, we where sitting down ,when he started to tell me why he was meeting me . You know he said , all the things you had to go through so far, in your life have been done to you for a reason , you have become very strong willed , also there is no fear of the unknown any more, where you are concerned right ? Yes that is thru , but why is this, why do we have to move so far away from our children, you know how much I love them ,this is the worst ,never in all my life did I leave anyone of them behind, now they all have to be left, may be this time my heart won't heal any more, it is broken in so many places, it cant mend any more . Don't talk such a nonsense, he said , just believe that God knows what he is doing , but first, you will have a lot of hard times ahead of you, for a long time , the only reason that he send me is as follows , He ,does not want you to loose your sense of humor , besides that , do not ever loose the happy go lucky self that we all had to come to love so much , he gave you that as a gift ,the greatest gift for any person to receive . Also, don't think that he has left you ,he would never do that , but there will be times when you will have the feeling that you are all alone in everything , be assured you are not , most of all , always keep an open mind as you have done so far ,it has brought you a long way , be nice to anybody as you have done when you where truly happy ,but happiness will return to you two fold . Naturally, you have to go through a lot of ups and down, more so now than ever before, stay well and know this , God loves you very much, he has always looked after you has he not ? Yes, he has ,but this is almost to much for me to bare ," don't be silly he said , you can do it, if anyone, it is you who is going to come out of this on the other side with flying colors , believe me . Remember, what I told you ,do not forget it , because these words will have to be your lifeline to us, and we do love you very much too and will always be around you okay ? That sounds great but I wish you all would be still here on earth with me I miss you all so much it hurts a lot ,sometimes . That is okay my sweet he said , you will do it we know , he just wanted me to be the one to talk to you , because he knew that it is going to be very hard for you to go this step . Waking up with a big ,sigh , my Husband asked me , what is wrong you have been turning around like made in bed, are you okay ? No not really , it was not the time to tell him about my dream , first I had to come to grips with all that was said to me . But how much harder could this get , wondering about that I did not go back to sleep, but got up, went to the Kitchenette and made myself a coffee , took that outside to sit on the balcony . For just a few minutes I had the strongest feeling my dad was sitting here with me ,even could smell his cigarettes , it was that distinct smell , because he always made his own cigarettes out of some kind of tobacco , that smelled very different form others . Taking a deep breath I said very quietly , okay dad I got your message, will do my best not to disappoint God or any one of you , love you , miss you a lot ! It was a very nice night, being the beginning of October very clear, and it seemed to me that some of the Stars where twinkling more brightly than before . It took me a while to realize that it was truly God who had send my dad to me, knowing that I always could believe him ,no matter what, he had a saying for me in every situation and he had gone through some very though times with me and the children after my Mother had died , he knew me very well . Sitting there , not seeing that day light was creeping up over the Mountain tops, when Peter got up I was still sitting there . What happened last night he asked , well may be we can talk about that on the way, right now it is too much to just talk about it okay ? He was fine with that ,he always knew when there was something very wrong , I would just close up for a while ,but not for long, after that he would find out what needed to be found out . Driving for about three hours , it was a nine hour drive to where we had to go, we had Senta our dog with us , at that time we had no cats, only her , she needed to go out and we stopped at this nice part in Washington State Park , we walked around for a while when I started telling Peter what kind of dream it was that had come to me in the night . He was listening until the end , looking at me, he said , your dad is right , you might have some very hard times ahead of you ,and you will be all alone at home for the first three years, I have to go around the globe so to speak a lot , not telling you this ,was not right, but it was the best for you ,because if I had told you may be you would not have come with me, right ? May be not ,I said, but it was not fair of you not telling me all that was involved , you know how being alone is not my thing . It will be okay he said, we buy a new Home for us there is going to be a lot of work to be done and it is going to keep your mind of the hurt and the missing the children . No, that is not how this works , no matter what you say, it is not how it works . Meanwhile we got back to the car the dog was happy now that she had gone for a walk, we wanted to stop in about two more hours , have some lunch . In the car I remembered all the paper work that had been found while cleaning out the desk , before moving , all the little notes that where made over the years ,and also, that so many times my wish had been to sit down and write some of the things down , things that happened to us over the years , both here and in Germany . There was a first thought ,about writing a book, not really a first thought but a for sure thought as I call it, now is the time . It was funny how those thoughts crept in to my mind ,but after a while I began to see what it was , this would be my time for writing books, for so many years wanting to start writing , I had not been ready, nor did I have the time ever , but now ,this was it ,may be that was what my dad was trying to tell me when he said , you will find out what you are supposed to do , and you will do it . Now was that time, and for the next few hours ,my thoughts where busy with the books, what ever they would be. But there definitely would be books , how come I was so sure about that was a mystery to me , but only for a little while , remembering my dads words brought back some of the things he had told me , at the end he had said , don't forget what has been said to you . He was right , may be there would be hard times but now there was a bit of light in the tunnel, not at the end of it , but a little bit was better than nothing . Had I known how hard it would be for me to be here alone , the first three years , probably my place would not have been here , we had bought an acreage , but there was no Garden, no flowers, nothing, it was a big challenge for me to work out here, loving to work outside, it must have been Gods will to send me here , there would be so much to do all the time, that one could not even look up to see the sun, just work . Some of the new Neighbors thought that I did not have a Husband, because for the first three years ,my Husband was mostly gone ,if he was home he had to sit in his Office planning the next trip . For all that they knew I was making up the fact , of having a Husband, so one day I decided to have a Garage Sale , never had one before, but the best thing of getting to know once neighbors would be just that .Sure enough a lot of them came we had a lot of talks about children ,husbands, Gardens , a lot of them where happy that we had moved in to this place, because now we had flower beds , the grass area was looking great , the former owner had nothing but Corn and Pumpkins growing here, he had been a Man living alone, there was no need for a big Vegetable garden . Not many People do have gardens around here, so when they saw my back yard they where in awe , we always see you working out here, where is your Husband ? Well right now he is in Germany but he will be home on the weekend , may be you can come by and meet him , so I told some of them , of course two of our next door neighbors had met my Husband on the first day that we had moved in, they had come over to welcome us to their neighborhood and told us a lot of stories about the Man who lived in this house before . About his family ,apparently he had a big Family too, six children or more, that was nice to know it must have been a happy home at one time . In the evenings there was nothing else to do but write, but it took me two more years before getting up the courage to send in my first Manuscript , it was a book about my Dog " Senta " she had been my best friend from the beginning, she was always by my side, even at night she would sleep sometimes at my feet on my bed , but mostly right next to my side of the bed on the floor . We have such a good relationship that now I don't have to tell her what she has to do just point or clap my hands, she does everything she is supposed to do . That book was a big hit with some of the Publisher's, most of them wanted a huge amount of money to publish my book , that was not what I had in mind , spending such an enormous amount was not in our budget, we needed to renovate this house, there was a lot that needed to be done I could not afford to spend that much . My husband had been right when he had told me ,that there would be a lot of work waiting for me here . But one day looking some of those Publisher's up on my Computer came across this one Authorhouse, who was not asking for so much, the only thing was one had to do their own Revisions and Public knowledge of the books or book as it was at that time . Now that was good news , right away I sat down and filled out the form they had in there, just like an application for a job, only this one was not as difficult to do . After two days the answer was , we love to Publish your book ,we had read it but it needs a bit of revision yet, if you could finish that and send it to us we have it out on the computer in no time at all . My first book, when telling my children the only one that was happy for me was my youngest son Peter, he loved that idea of having a book out that his Mother had written ,but my three older children where not so happy ,they had hoped that I would wither away over here ,because they where all mad at me for moving away in the first place, it was very sad . Today there are four books out that where written by me, this is number fiver , and I hope that it is the lucky number that it always has been for me . God has guided me through Hell and high water , there is no doubt in my mind, but remembering my father telling me that , the once God loves the most , he will test the most, they have to go through a lot just to find out if they are truly believers ,and this one is, to this day, God is my guidance , my strength, he gives me so much to look forward to for the next day, he has given me a gift that was my wish from when I was about twelve years old, the wish to write books. It has taken a long time, but then we all know, that God takes his time, he does not go by the hours of our watches, he has his own good time, but he will bring us the happiness we deserve as soon as we have proven to him that he is the only one for us, and always will be till our death. With me, he is the one and only, he knows that, and there is nobody and nothing that can change my mind, going through some rough times has made me stronger, it has shown me that there is so much I can do, never having thought it would be possible for me, to do all that I have done up to now. There is one, last event that happened just a few months ago. My Sister had, died in Germany, nobody from my family notified me, I had no way of knowing that she was not around any more. Having had this sister who always did, something to make me look very bad, she would say all kinds of things to me when she was at our House for a visit from Germany. Many of our Friends told me so often not to let her come to us any more, to visit, because all she did most at the time was call me names, the once I do not like to repeat, also tell me as often as she could that I was a no good for nothing, person, who thinks that, because she believes in God, was better than her. But none of those things did matter to me, she was my sister and as such I did love her, id was okay if she was not to nice to me, she had a bad life, we all knew that it had made her miserable, so, she was not the best person to have around. Not to say the least, the last time she came here was in 2001 shortly before her 65^{fth} Birthday, knowing about her special day and also being aware that nobody in Germany had given her any kind of party what so ever, I had planned the whole day without her knowing , a nice party for her .Even had invited some of our Neighbors and friends to make it a very nice evening for her . She was complaining to me all day because I was in the Kitchen the whole time, but being November , it was raining outside from morning to night fall ,so it really did not matter what I would be doing , we could not go outside and she did not want to go to the Mall either . Her complaining held on until about eight o'clock that night ,when my son asked her to go to the store with him for cigarettes ,that way we could Decorate , the dining area and kitchen, set the table and so on . My husband said that I was crazy to do anything for her, but like I said , she was my sister and I did love her . When they got back the visitors where here already the house was decorated with balloons and so on, she was looking very surprised and asked me , this you did for me , for my birthday ? Yes, this is all for your birthday ,you telling me that you did all the cooking and baking all day today just for me, and you let me go on complaining about this ? Yes, I did , why is it such a crime to do something for once sister ? No she said but you of all people did this for me ,I can not believe this , not even my children had send me a card let alone give me a party, they did not even phone me, on my day . Well now you will have a great party tonight and have fun , happy birthday I said , going towards her giving her a big hug , we also had a nice gift for here she had told us that her last Watch was broken on the way coming here from Germany in the Air Plain and so we had gotten her a new Watch a very nice one at that . For the first time I saw tears in her eyes , she did not cry like we would have, but her eyes where watery, she did not say thank you, but the look she gave me was good enough for me . Than just before Christmas 2006 exactly on December, 24 I got a Letter from her Landlord ,who had opened her Postal box at the house she was living in . Since I did not know that she had passed away I had send her a Birthday Card also Christmas Cards from us and my children and some letters ,you see we where having her come to live with us . She had been asking me about that the, Christmas before , since she did not have not very much money, she needed someone to let her live with them so she would not have to pay Rent . Her two Children, both Married ,and having a nice house, did not want her to come live there . Finding this out I was the one who told her she could come to live with us, as soon as we had cleared this with the American Authorities . Now that, we had done , it was October 2006 , we could ask her to come ,we even made arrangements to have her dog come with her on the Plain . We had not talked to her since that last April, when I had told her that she could come to live here, she was very happy, but did not tell me that she had gotten worst , her health was very bad but like I said we could not know . The only thing that we told her was , we would phone her as soon as we got the Papers ready for her to come and live here with us . But sadly enough, neither ,one of her children, nor my other sisters thought to inform me about this , that she had passed away in August that year 2006. Having gotten everything ready for her to move in here I wrote her the letter telling her that all was ready for her to come over, not knowing that she could not answer any more ,but I was wondering why her phone did not work any more, trying to explain that as to the fact she might have it disconnected already, since she was coming here . Any way, on December 24, which is our Christmas Eve , we got that letter from her Landlord , telling me that they where very sorry, but needed to let me know that my sister had passed away ,she had , had a third stroke and did not feel to much pain but she died very alone . Reading this it was unbelievable to me that any one could be so cruel as to leave her to die alone , finding out from same landlord that her Daughter new she was in the Hospital so did her son but neither of them would go to see her . Looking up to the sky as I was standing outside , I needed to talk to God about this ,it was to much for me to handle, we had gotten ready to have lunch, but I told me Husband just to go ahead ,my appetite was gone ,tears where filling my eyes . On a day like today, we had to find out about this , how can my own family be so cruel , not to let me know ,they all knew that she would be coming here if she had been better ,she had made no secret out of that, I even had phone calls from her kids, not to let her come here, she would make my life miserable, but telling them that she needed someone from her family who would be there for her, that was more important to me than all the other things . It took me four months to come to grips with this , always asking God , why , if you are truly the loving Father you say you are in the Bible , why then, let her die like that, it was not fair , besides ,you did not even let me say good by to her . It was the same prayer every day, than about four weeks ago it was a good day ,a very good friend of mine had asked me the day before if she could pick me up the next morning, she would like for me to go shopping with her and out to lunch . We had a very good time and I did not think of my sister one bit that whole day . When that night , a very nice Dream was had by me . Going through the Forest at my house here, in my dream , my sister was coming towards me , she looked very nice, not sick at all ,she was dressed in a very nice light colored Dress, she was very skinny ,like she used to be when she was young , coming towards me with a great big smile, than stopping right in front of me . Hi little sister, she said , how are you , do not worry about me any more , I am fine ,it is very good where I am now , Mom & Dad say hi too and so do our brothers and sister , just needed to come to tell you that I am so sorry to have been such a bad sister to you , can you ever forgive me ? Sure , it is okay there is nothing to forgive ,the only thing that I can not get over is the fact that God did not give me the chance to say good by to you, at least give you a big hug on the way . Always loved you but you know that by now right ? Oh yes, she said, now I do know a lot of things God gave me this chance to talk to you about this I need to let you know that I am truly sorry for always being so mean to you , you know God is truly as you have always told me he would be .But I have to go now and wont come back, but will you please forgive me, and I do love you and now you have one more angel to look out for you . With that she was gone and I woke up , my pillow was wet and I needed to change it , so getting up very quietly went in to the living room and sat down . What had just happened ? That dream was just like it had been real , my sisters hug felt so warm and real ,the things she said where so sincere , how could that be ,it was not just because I wanted it that way, but because she was truly saying good by to me . How lucky for her , she now was with my Parents , with my brothers and my sister who had died a long time ago , why could I not be there to see them all , asking God this question I felt like he was not very happy with me that moment . By the time I was going back to bed I could hear the alarm going of from our clock , my husband was just getting up . How long had I been sitting there ? It was clear to me that my sister had appeared to me in that dream ,because she and I had never had the chance to say good by , God had given us the opportunity, to do that in the dream . All felt so real, because it was real , to me, and to her , because by the Grace of God ,we had been able to say our sorry and our good bys ! Now making breakfast for my husband I was not sure if to tell him or not, but he knew that there was something wrong , he had noticed me getting up in the middle of the night . Did you have on of those dreams again he asked , yes I did , this time it was my sister ,she had told me that she was sorry for all she had done to me , and that she loved me ,she even gave me a big hug, it felt so warm and she had never given me a hug in all my life . It must mean something because, by the grace of God ,she was able to come back to let me know how she really felt , I am sure of that . Are you going back to bed after I leave , you haven't got very much sleep , may be, but not sure . But going back to bed sounded pretty good to me at this point and after my husband had left I did go to have some sleep . The only thing was, this time I dreamed again ,only this time it was my brother Harry , who was the main person in that dream . Because having sat up most of the night thinking about my family, Parents and brothers, now two sisters, who all have died , it was probably natural to be dreaming about this ,but it was a dream I had many times before ,the only difference was , this time, it was not quit the same . Arriving at the House my Parents live in ,the, one in my dream that I had visited may times already, my Mother had opened the door , giving me a hug and kisses on my cheeks , she let me inside but instead of going to the living room where we always had coffee, we walked to the foot of the stair case, where she called my brother Harry . Could you please show her the room that is going to be hers

, she said , " of course Mom he said , taking me by the hand we walked up a long flight of stairs , which was followed by an equal long hallway, at the end of that there where plastic sheets hanging from the Ceiling to the floor, but before we got there he asked me if I would like to see the rooms where he and my other siblings lived . Sure that would be great , opening one door after the other, all the rooms where very nice , lots of light , by having great big windows, and decorated perfectly . Now we get to your room he said ,lifting one of the plastic sheets aside he pointed ahead of me , look he said this is going to be your room , but it is not finished yet ,I said, why is it not done up like all the others ? Well, it is not time for you, to come to live here yet , you must wait till it is your time, but by then your room will be ready . Tears where flowing again , but I want to come here now, to live, it is very lonely where I am , without all of you , sometimes it is too much for me to bare, the pain of missing all of you . But you have done so well , he said , and there is much to do for you yet, believe me , it is not your time yet ,also you know by now that we are all there around you, even if you can't see us all the times ,but we are there, remember what we told you many years ago . You had seen us with the Coyotes, haven't you , what did we tell you then ." That you would always be there with me and as long as I keep you in my heart , I have you with me wherever I go ! " That is all well but sometimes I wish you would be right next to me ,so I could talk to you, and not have to wait for a dream to visit all of you . Listen he said , do not be un great full , you have a great life, and you have been give a great gift, do not throw that away , we will be waiting here for you no matter how long it takes , besides ,we need to make your room just like you would like it okay ? That is good , I could hear myself saying, but my heart was not in this , it would have been much better for me to have been able to stay there ,but knowing that they all are there and having no pain, instead, having a great existence , it was doing my heart good to know that . Waking up was always a downer , it had been such a warm environment and now I felt totally exhausted . It was always that way ,when waking up after one of those dreams , to this day I do not know why that is ,but it must have a reason . When I was told by my Brother , that my time had not come yet and my room was not ready , it felt like loosing them all over again , but of course it was not so and in time , coming to grips with what was known to me now , it mad all perfectly sense . It does not matter if we believe that or not, it does matter that God has his hands over us ,and he is the one who guides us , many times people have said to me , but why is God letting all those bad things happen . Why , because we take everything for granted , most of us do not truly believe as the Bible say's believe like a babe , look at the children, most of them believe with all their heart, but then when we grow up, we loose that because we have seen so much bad things happen ,that it we think it could not be the will of God , but guess what , it is his will and when we pray , your will be done , than that should be enough for us to know that praying like that is giving him the right to have his will be done . Most of us believe, that we should have our own life in our hands but with so many people doing that, we can see what is happening all over the world , nobody believes in God any more or Allah or whatever we call him, he might have a lot of names but he is the only one, who truly has our best interest at Heart .We must get back to basics, or we loose all he has ever given us . Instead of being great full, we complain most at the time ,we put the blame on others because that is the easy way out, why should we take the blame for our own misfortune when we can say things like , we have no part in this ,we did not do anything ,or , we had a very bad childhood ,now everybody in this world has to pay for that . We do not heed his words ,when he tells us , he who has killed by the sword must also be killed by the sword . Nobody looks at those words, and we condemn the people or countries who still live by his rules , we fight them with all we got , we do not see that they have not forgotten his words . Very sad to see, that so many children in our days are not believers, they should be made aware of his presents, not that I will go out now to preach ,that is not my assignment , but when I was growing up , believing was the biggest part of my life, always, and still is today . Sometimes, I had wandered of the beat and path , not knowing what to believe because of all the bad things that happened to me, but I always found my way back to him, no matter what , he always took me back , no questions asked , just be there and wait for me to repent, that is what God is all about ,the ever loving Father . Even if he is harsh sometimes , he has to be , we do not listen to anything but bad news on television, so if that is the way he gets our attention than so be it , a lot of us do not believe that God can also punish us, if we do not repent ,to those I say , look at Sodom and Gomorrah what happened there , look at the City they recovered just a few years ago, who had been under dust and ashes, for many years , I could count of more than that ,but by now you all have gotten the idea of what is being told to you here, right ? Just keep in mind that without God nobody would be here and if he chooses all of this could be gone at the snip of a finger , nobody would ever know, that we had been here , is that what you all want out of life ? For my part it is not , that is why believing in him is very important to me,, I have been called crazy ,because I say what I think, but that is the gift he gave ,me never to have to say something that is not thru, always telling it like it is . My Father and Mother have thought me that way when telling and teaching me about the Bible ,and thank God , my parents where that way ,it has given me a lot of good things in life and the sad parts are all part of that life as well, if not for crying, we could not be laughing either ,so lets keep the faith and hope and stand fast , so when he calls on you ,there is no fear of meeting him , but only happiness ,okay ? Besides , there is no need for fear, nobody truly knows, but we do have to account for what we have done with our life, that is certain, but he is very forgiving and we should be too . Knowing a lot of people who go to Church every Sunday , but never feel the need to be nice to People , or forgive anybody who has said or done something to them in the past , plus they do not know the word kindness , all they know is, what the one guy in church got , the car he was driving today ,or , how much money he made in the past year . They talk about God, but only use him for an excuse to do things we would not do, like Gossip about people, even if they do not know all the facts, they take it upon themselves to place judgment on others and do not care who they hurt in the process . Those kind of people we should stay away from , but we have no right to judge them either, that is up to God ,he will deal with them in his own good time ,as he always does . The only once we should be concerned with is our self ,do what is right , not kill anybody , don't steal from your neighbor and most of all , help whoever calls on you for help and you will have a good life, that is his promise to us ,who believe in him .For myself , if the day comes when I have to stand before him , it will be the best thing for me , not because I have been an Angel all my life , far from it , but because he is forgiving , he loves me very much , like he does all of his children , he also wants us to admit what we have done wrong, so he can make it right for us . He has done so much for me in all the years that I have been praying to him , always kept my children safe from any bad thing that could have happened to them, without having them live by only his word , he always brought my Husband back to me save from any Trip he had to go on . We all do get the chance to do what we think , even if it turns out to be wrong , he lets us make those kind of mistakes because we all have to learn ,that , if a mistake has been made, than that is our own doing not his. The only thing is that he can make it right for us if we want him to and ask him for help . In all the years of my life, he has done nothing that could have truly hurt me , my Mother dying was good for her , but we as humans always want to keep everybody and everything for us , never do we want anybody to go away that we love . But we do not think about them , just about ourselves , and that is selfish , if you ask me . For one I have been very much so, for a few years until some people , like my now Husband Peter who truly loved me ,put me in the right direction again, but without Gods help I would not have survived those years . The reason he let me through there was to make me stronger , coming out at the other end ,he knew the things that would wait for me in my future ,only he could have known them . Also, that my wish was to write from when I was still in great School , but never had the time , raising four children having a full time job and looking after my Husband actually the whole family all the time, was enough work for me . Never had time to do what my wish had been, the one I had asked him for a long time ago , to be a Writer , he knew when the time was right, that my wish would come thru ,and it has . Not that the money is that important to me , oh no , it never was , the only thing was, that there was and is so much to write about, which People would like to know, that someone has to do it even if that person should be myself !

    Having found a very good husband , actually who has found me because it was Gods will , we now are married for 33 years and hopefully with the blessing of God the almighty ,we will make it to our 50 anniversary and stay together . Throughout the whole 33 years we had some ups and downs but most of all we always stuck it out together , too many people give up , if it comes to some miss understandings , or to whatever it is they do not like ,even if it is that one of the partners goes to wrong way once , we should make sure that Love is the main thing in our life , always remember why you married that other person ,what attracted you to that one partner ? If you ever forget that then go apart, but if you remember , than , stay together, work at it , the rewards are so much more than one could expect .But the main ingredient is , pray to God , he is the one who holds all the cards he can give or take it away from us ,be sure to say thank you to him, if given some very special times ,or things that you wanted . Never forget who is the one and only that looks after you, even when nobody else wants you , he will be there for you . Don't ever, forget that you are not the only person in this world , if you want respect from anybody else than you have to give that respect , if it is love , you have to give that as well . No matter what it is, if you do not give ,you never get either, that is his first commandment , to give and if you are doing that without being sorry that

you have given anything , you will find out how much more happiness you get in return .Just try it for a little while , find out for yourselves what it is he has to offer ,you might be very pleasantly surprised . After all the ups and downs in my life ,arriving at this time , it is so rewarding for me to see how much I have accomplished , but not because I had been the smartest person ,or the most intelligent ,but because he let me be what I wanted to be without having to sell my soul to anybody . Always stayed on the right path , His , even in hard times thinking of him was enough for him , he still did not leave me alone , he was there even after all the bad things . He let me deal with it in my own way, but he also knew , that on the other end , there was the person he wanted me to be, and that to me is the best thing that could have ever happened to me ! Hoping that whit this book some of you might see more clearly what you should do , or how you should change some things , but do not make the mistake of thinking you can do it on your own , ask him for his help , he is always waiting for some of us to ask him for help, for guidance ,please do ask him and you find out what I have already a long time ago . Now at this time in my life , a great deal of thanks goes to my Parents, even if they are not here with me any more, I do believe he lets them know how I felt, and feel right now , they know that , the things they thought me and the love they gave me has made me to a person that is now happy, and has a lot to offer to anybody, who likes to be a friend to me, because I do not wait to get anything ,but give freely to my friends, without asking rewards back, and that is the secret . Do not ask for anything, just give ,like I said before ,the things you get in return are much more valuable than Gold or Silver , no money in the world can buy you a thru Friend, but your friendship ,can make a very good friend happy, and help him if need to be . Let me say this at the end , if I could do my life over again there is nothing that I would change , all the sad things , all the happy things and events have made who I am now , having had to go through a lot ,has made me see that it is not I that has achieved all that I have today ,but just by the," Grace of God " have I gotten this far and ,for the rest of my life I will thank him for my life , he has given me so much . Having been told at the age of nineteen , that my life would be ending at the age of twenty three , was not good , having been a Baby ,that had come in to this world very sick, and having had to spend the first three months of my life in a Hospital, was hard on my Parents . Also , surviving the time limit given to me earlier , but than being told by several doctors that there would never be the joy of having children for me . When in fact ,at twenty three, there where Claudia , Dieter , and Joerg Ren'e in my life , it was God who granted me my wishes . In all those years, that was what I prayed for, every day every night , sometimes several times during the day , when others told me that I was crazy to think my life would be good , he was there , to show me that it was very good at times . Now, asking all of you , can you say that from anybody else , can anyone do those kind of things for you ? Guess not , but if you believe in him and his Son , you will find out that things are going to happen to you, that not in your wildest dreams would you have believed would happen . And sometimes you will ask your self , is it truly him who is doing this for me , than just look up in to the Heavens and even on a cloudy day , you will feel this happy feeling, coming over you , but you have to give him all your trust, without that he can not help you .

Today some of my children do not talk to me any more, but even that is a time that he has decided on for me , as it turns out , for once, did I speak out after twenty years of having heard the abuse from my own children ,who where saying not such good things about me . Sure an Angel I was not, but nobody has the right to speak ill of me ,least of all my own children ,because all my life had revolved around them ,if there was ever any one in need for anything I was there, some of my friends have told me not to do so much for my ,children because they would never thank me for it . They do not realize that I am not looking for thank you from them , the only thing I ever wanted was their respect ,their love, that was all, nothing more or less , but neither one of my oldest children seem to be able to give that to me . Only my youngest Son, Peter junior , he is such a great Man ,at his age he has never said anything bad to me, nor has he ever been disrespectful, nor in ,any way said anything to offend me . He always shows me his love by telling me ,

Mom I love you, look after yourself because I want you in my life for a long time to come ! He did not want to talk to my other children any more but that was not what I had in mind , always telling him , they are your Brothers and sister , do not judge them, ever , tell them that you love them ,be nice to them , encourage them if they need to be , but most of all , remember not to forget them because in the end you might need them to be there for you or they might need you . Now does that sound familiar to any one of you out there , it was the same thing my Mother had always told me many years ago about my own siblings . The reason I wrote this is , hearing of so many siblings who do not speak to one another , please do not do that, it is not Gods will that you behave like that , try to understand what they need and even if they do not want any part of you ,at least you have tried and that is the main thing . Hoping for all of you who read this that you be happy , God Bless you and keep you save at all times . The last and final episode of how God works his wonders is as follows , knowing that a lot of People do not believe in God or not in wonders that he can bring us, here is one , nobody has ever been able to explain to me how much some of them have tried ! We had bought an old Ford Truck that we wanted to use to bring our Garbage away in , living out in the Country we could just bury it but that was never our intention ,because it would pollute the ground in time . Having had a bit of work to do on said Truck we had it in a Garage for three days after that we went to buy new tires for it and than it was off to Canada with it . We had remodeled our House and taken out a lot of the old doors which my Son wanted to restore , but since he lived in Canada that was where I had to go . Never had taken this Truck out before but now it seemed to be an adventure because I had to cross two Mountain Passes, pretty high once too. The Mechanic, that had repaired our Truck ensured me that it would be okay to drive it over the Mountains and back, his words,' this truck takes you to the end of the earth if you want it too. Having had two new Batteries put in the vehicle would prove to be a mistake. Any way, all the way to my sons place in Canada, which is about an eight to ten hour drive from where we lived in Washington State, was okay but I could smell some foul odor coming from the front. First believing that it was the big Highway Truck ahead of me, I did not pay to much attention to the matter and arriving at my sons house had him look at the Motor just to see if he could find anything wrong with it. He did not and after two days I was on my way back to the States, to Battle Ground to be exact. Now the first pass is the highest when coming away from Kelowna Canada, Kelowna meaning ,Grizzly Bear, having mastered the first big pass it was all the way down from there until just before Vancouver Canada, at the tip of that pass was a toll booth but before reaching it I needed to let my dog go out for a bit of a walk. Coming back from our walk my Truck did not start any more, no matter what I did it was useless. Now I began to worry to top this off, my cell phone did not work either, all the numbers I tried nothing ,not a noise what so ever. Finally after having tried all the numbers that I could, tried the 911, the Lady on the other end told me that she was not in charge of stuck Trucks or not working vehicles as she said it, 'you have to phone the Road Service. Madam I said, after trying all the numbers yours is the only one that got through, how do you explain that. Where about are you located, she asked, well I am just below the Toll Booth at that last rest stop. Wait she said , I will phone the triple AAA and send them to you , what does your truck look like . After giving an exact description I hang up the phone , sitting there waiting for the road service to get to me would take over one hour they had to come from the last city that I had passed ,with was Merrit right in between a group of Mountains . While waiting I went outside to walk my dog a bit more it was very early still and some other cars where parked there which the people where sleeping in . Thinking about the Truck and what it could be that did not want to work I was thinking of the Batteries but since they had been brand new that could not be it , or could it ? Well after about an hour and half the tipple AAA guy arrived , he parked right next to me . Putting, the dog in to the, back of the truck so that the Man could try to start my car, he was asking me what happened . Well on my way to Kelowna I smelled a foul odor coming from the front, like rotten eggs , but after a while it stopped so paying no attention to that any more went on to get to my sons house . But this morning driving up the first Mountain pass it started again but this time it was worst than the first time . Hello , he said we do not have to look any more , he opened the hood and looked at the two batteries , they are not new he said ,besides whoever put these in there , did not fill them up with water . Now that was news to me, that a Mechanic would put in a battery not checking it if the water was in there , even I knew that one had to check once in an while some people do some don't but I for one and my husband we always did check everything before going on a trip . Only this time because the Mechanic had done a good, job , so I thought we did not make sure if everything was okay . You know Madam , this nice Man said , you could have gone up to Heaven this morning already

, why is that I asked him , well with both batteries not having any water this truck could have exploded , like I have seen may of them do, since I work along the highway he said to me . It is a wonder that you could go to your sons and come back to here and not have the Truck fly to pieces all ,over , you can thank your lucky stars honestly ! Not my lucky stars I thought , but God , he knew from the start that there was something wrong but he brought me where I needed to go and back here at least he let me phone the one number that would help, the 911 , telling some of our friends and most of all to my Husband who is an Mechanical Engineer , he told me that I could be glad to be alive . Knowing that now I always make sure that my car is in good order and everything is working on it ,but not to worry to much because I know that one is always there to help , God , he has not let me down yet and he never will I do believe that with all my heart ! He has made me see that without him there is nothing at all , but if we believe in him even going through some very rough times, makes it easier for us not to loose hope . There was a time when I did not talk to him or listen to my inner voice ,and in those times I had to endure a lot of pain and heart ship ,but when talking to him about that, it all seemed to fade away and it was not really that bad , at least it did not seem that way . Now after having had all the prove that I needed to know he was always there with me I can walk through any darkness, knowing that only he is the one who can shed light on my life and he does . Sometimes when life gets to be a bit much even for me I go and sit outside , not looking up ,but still talking to him telling him that I do not like this feeling , that I am not willing to have those kind of feelings , than something funny happens , either the phone rings and it is one of my friends or my children who need some help with something or one of my neighbors is at the door asking for some kind of help . Right, then , it makes me forget what I had been moping about and give any advise freely , if I know about that particular problem , if not , I try to help any way that my ability lets me help . To this day there has been a lot of sadness in my life but also a lot of happiness , when one is the youngest of ten children it is only normal that the older once die first unless there is an accident in which case it is twice as hard for the once who are left behind . But in my case it has been the norm that all my siblings have died before me since I am the youngest it is very sad for me , if before I could say , I can ask my sister or my brother about this or my Parents , now that is no more , there is no one left for me to ask anything concerning my younger years ,and it is very hard at times , but even in my darkest hour , God seemed to know what I needed always and even if it was just someone coming to the house collecting Groceries for the food bank or the poorer people, he always told me not to be such a cry baby , that there are people out there who are much worst of than I was . This is the sole reason this book has been written , for all of you out there who despair , don't do that , instead , sit down anywhere you like and talk to him, tell him what is bothering you right now , and you find out that within a short time you feel that he has helped you no matter how but he has ! For my person and my family , I can honestly say that , most times we talk about the thing that bothers us the most , if we have an argument we talk it over and it becomes so insignificant that we laugh about it after a while . What I have learned most of all , to talk about any problem no matter what it is , talk it over with your loved one ,or once make sure that they do understand that you did not mean any harm when voicing your opinion to them even if they misunderstood what you had been trying to say . After it has been talked about there is no misunderstanding any more and all is well with the world .

About the Author

This Author has been writting for a long time but it took about twelve years before she finally got the courage to have a Publisher look at one of her Manuscripts , she was told that it was a good Book , now she has several on the Market . This one is truly after her own Life ,ups and downs come in to everybodys life and very often she followed not her Heart but what she was told by her Husband she should follow, but what turned out to be the wrong way . Now she has her own life back and is convinced that with this Book she can help so many People find their own way to what is truly important .

Monika Grunwald-Schutz

Printed in the United States
123052LV00002B/181/P